Power Encounters

Other books by John Wimber with Kevin Springer

Power Evangelism
Power Healing
Study Guide to Power Healing

Power Encounters
Among Christians in the Western World

Compiled and Edited by
Kevin Springer

With an Introduction and Afterword by
John Wimber

1817

Harper & Row, Publishers, San Francisco

Cambridge, Hagerstown, New York, Philadelphia, Washington
London, Mexico City, São Paulo, Singapore, Sydney

FIRST EDITION

Library of Congress Cataloging-in-Publication Data

Power encounters among Christians in the western world.

  1. Evangelism—History—20th century.
2. Christianity—20th century.   I. Springer, Kevin.
BR1640.P69   1988   269   87-45724
ISBN 0-06-069537-4

88   89   90   91   92   MPC   10   9   8   7   6   5   4   3   2   1

To Ray Nethery, my pastor, mentor, and friend.

"Perfume and incense bring joy to the heart, and the pleasantness of one's friend springs from his earnest counsel." (Prov. 27:9)

Contents

Acknowledgments

Working with sixteen writers who are scattered across four continents could have been an editorial disaster. They might have been slow to respond (or not responded at all!) to the many requests that accompany the writing of a book. Instead, all of my requests received their immediate attention, and the result was a group of stories that weave together like a fine tapestry. I thank all the writers for their willingness to write about intimate details of their lives, for it is difficult to expose our souls to people we may never meet.

Two people deserve special recognition, for without their help *Power Encounters* could never have been written. The first is C. Peter Wagner, of Fuller Theological Seminary, whose story appears in the book and whose thinking about power encounters and the Third Wave permeates all the writings. Dr. Wagner made many valuable suggestions and was especially helpful in supplying data that supported key theses in my foreword and John Wimber's introduction and afterword.

Of course, without John Wimber's support this book could never have been written, both because of his encouragement to the contributors and because of his ministry in their lives. His outstanding introduction and afterword frame the living portraits, providing the reader with a broader understanding of what the Holy Spirit is doing in our day. This is our fourth book project together, and each one has been a privilege and joy to be a part of.

Finally, my wife Suzanne, editor of *The Vineyard Newsletter,* read every chapter and offered suggestions that greatly strengthened the book. In all that I do she is my partner and "a wife of noble character" (Prov. 31:10).

Kevin Springer
January 1988
Yorba Linda, California

Foreword: What Is a Power Encounter?

When I entitled this book *Power Encounters Among Christians in the Western World,* I was aware of missiologists' more technical use of the term "power encounter." But I believed the term also could be used in a broader, less technical way to describe encounters of Western Christians with the Holy Spirit, encounters that dramatically change their worldview and practice. I met with C. Peter Wagner of Fuller Seminary, and he agreed with me. In this foreword I define how I am using the term "power encounter," so as not to confuse it with its more technical meaning.

In our book *Power Evangelism,* John Wimber and I describe power encounters as the clashing of the kingdom of God with the kingdom of Satan. "Any system or force that must be overcome for the gospel to be believed," we write, "is cause for a power encounter" (p. 16). *Any system or force that must be overcome* in Western culture usually involves a worldview that denies the supernatural. To understand how forces in our culture work against belief in the supernatural, we must take a closer look at the influence of Enlightenment thinking.

Paganism

Harold Lindsell, in his book *The New Paganism,* traces the influence of the eighteenth-century Enlightenment on Western culture up to today. Here is his summary:

The Enlightenment did not arise, peak, and decline like some other movements. Rather it became more widespread, moving forward and gaining momentum subsequent to the end of the eighteenth century. It was not to reach its full flowering until after the middle of the twentieth century, at which time its impact could be seen in the defeat of the church in the West. . . .

The Enlightenment's opposition to metaphysics, its denial of the supernatural, and its exaltation of reason over revelation found its classical expression in a world and life view (Weltanschauung) wholly inconsonant with historic orthodoxy; this was accompanied by an intellectual, moral, and cultural climate (Zeitgeist) in accord with this pagan world and life view. This meant that the West had lost its Judeo-Christian foundations and was now thoroughly pagan, although it did not mean that the Christian faith was obliterated. Rather it was a minority viewpoint in a society that was governed by paganism. The West had become pluralistic and was marked by two major viewpoints in opposition to each other, but the controlling viewpoint was pagan and anti-Christian (p. 90).

Enlightenment thinking has so permeated Western culture that Western culture is no longer "Christian in any significant way. . . . The prevailing Weltanschauung [worldview] today in America and in Europe is pagan" (p. 116).

John Wimber, in the introduction to this volume, has much more to say about the influence of the Enlightenment on Western society and, particularly, on the thinking of Christians. For the purposes of defining how I use the term "power encounter," though, *the Enlightenment's most significant influence among Christians is to bend their thinking away from the supernatural and toward rationalism and materialism.*

Crises

I divide the testimonies into different sections, based on the doorways through which the writers pass for their power encounters. They include personal encounters, doctrinal encounters, pastoral encounters, missionary encounters, and, in a few instances, conscious worldview encounters. I will have more to say about each of these doorways at the beginning of each section.

Few Christians are conscious of their worldview; they rarely question it. But sometimes a crisis arises that turns their world upside down, causing them to reexamine how they look at it. Under these circumstances they reconsider their view of God and themselves. These crises are opportunities for the Holy Spirit to work in their lives—doorways to renewal that lead the participants to a power encounter.

Phenomena associated with power encounters vary, ranging from dramatic dreams that reveal serious personal sin to physical healings. In almost every instance there is a new awareness of personal unbelief and sin, so deep a revelation that it quite literally shakes the recipient. For all, the outcome is a new dependency on God, faith in God's supernatural acting today, and new dimensions of ministry—in sum, a new worldview that allows more freely and fully for God's supernatural intervention in the everyday affairs of men and women.

In terms of concrete changes of behavior, all whose stories you are about to hear now regularly pray for the sick, have a more lively and intimate prayer life, and are more effective teachers and preachers. Further, the power encounters in these individuals have affected many others. Whole families and congregations have been renewed and, in some cases, are growing. In this regard power encounters among Christians in Western culture are quite similar to power encounters among those in non-Western cultures. Perhaps as you read these stories you too will be touched by the power of the Holy Spirit and experience the blessing of a power encounter that will change your life.

Tippett and Wagner

This understanding of power encounters, however, differs from missiologists' understanding of it in non-Western cultures. (Missiologists are experts on the field of Christian missions.) To understand how the word is used by missiologists, we must turn to the writings of Alan R. Tippett and C. Peter Wagner. Wagner defines a power encounter as "a visible, practical demonstration that Jesus Christ is more powerful than the spirits, powers, or false gods worshiped or feared by the members of a given people group." Power encounters are direct confrontations between the forces of good and evil. They are usually public events, resulting in group conversions. Many missiologists believe power encounters are a factor contributing to the remarkable growth of Christianity in many Third World countries.

All conversions involve some form of power encounter, but people movements (where groups of people convert at the same time and where the group conversion has great impact on their non-Christian relatives) often involve overt confrontations between the forces of good and evil. These groups, usually found in animistic cultures, shift their allegiance to Christ, and, so far as their culture is concerned, they risk retribution from spirits, demons, and deities that their societies recognize as controlling the affairs of daily life. This dynamic then creates a fertile environment for further power encounters.

Alan Tippett has written extensively on power encounters in two books, *Solomon Islands Christianity* and *People Movements in Southern Polynesia*. In *People Movements in Southern Polynesia*, Tippett draws on his twenty years of experience as a missionary in the Fiji Islands to make these observations:

In presenting the gospel the missionary advocated a plan of salvation. Much of this his hearers needed no convincing of. Sin and fear were real. They understood the need of salvation. They did not doubt the power of the God about whom the missionaries spoke. They knew that power (mana) to save had to come from outside themselves. If the advocates of Christianity could offer something better than the religion they had followed they were interested. But the superiority of that salvation had to be proved by practical demonstration. Somewhere there had to be an actual encounter between Christ and the old god. To the Pacific islander this was best done by means of his own act of faith—an ocular demonstration of a change of loyalty. This encounter is the key to the first stage of missionary activity, the stage that brings the pagan across the line into the Christian camp. Those historians and other scholars who have scoffed at mission work because of the material accompaniments of conversion have completely missed this key to the missionary situation—the fundamentality of dynamic encounter (pp.160–61).

The best scriptural example of the type of power encounter Tippett and Wagner speak of is found in 1 Kings 18:20–40, the story of Elijah on Mount Carmel. Elijah challenged four hundred and fifty prophets of Baal in an open confrontation: my God versus your God; whoever is left standing at the end is the winner. This was high drama, an ancient "shootout at the OK Corral." In the end, only the God of Abraham, Isaac, and Jacob was left standing; Baal was routed. In response to this dramatic victory the people turned to God proclaiming, "The Lord—he is God! The Lord—he is God!"

Paul's confrontation of Elymas the sorcerer in Acts 13 is a New Testament example of a power encounter. Elymas's influence was a formidable barrier keeping Sergius Paulus, the Roman proconsul, from becoming a Christian. But after Elymas was blinded by Paul's words, Sergius Paulus believed in Christ. Why? Because "he was amazed at the teaching about the Lord." That teaching was embodied in the demonstration that Paul's God was superior to Elymas's god.

When defined this way, power encounters have generally occurred today with people groups in non-Western cultures, usually in the Third World. The God of the Bible overcomes demons, powers, and false gods that have enslaved the people, a supernatural enslavement the people were conscious of. And because of group solidarity, usually many members if not the entire group are converted as a result of this emancipation. One key to understanding why power encounters are so effective in non-Western cultures is they overcome taboos and in so doing demonstrate the superiority of Christianity in terms people understand and accept.

For example, Tippett points out that the Samoans believed "that the only real and effective way of proving the power of their new faith was to demonstrate that the old religion had lost its powers and fears" (*People Movements in Southern Polynesia*, p. 164). To illustrate how power encounters demonstrate that superiority, Tippett recounts the story of Malietoa and his family:

Malietoa had accepted Fauea and the teachers, had cared for them and built them a chapel. The day before its opening he assembled his family, for it was on the family level that he had determined to act. He announced his intention of becoming a follower of the Christian God. The family, after discussion, approved. Socially all was correctly done; but in his own mind he was still not quite certain, and therefore determined to exclude his sons from the experiment. They were to wait and see how things turned out for their father and the members of the family who shared the experiment with him. Again the matter was debated and the family decided on a four-to-six weeks test. If all went well then the sons would follow. It was a communal decision.

It would seem then that the natural point for power encounter was the reverence and taboo of the *aitu* [an object or animal in which their god was thought to dwell]. . . . Their health, their security, their prosperity, their perpetuity all depended on the reverence and observation of taboos connected with their *aitu*. To desecrate, destroy, or devour one's *aitu* required a real act of faith in some power greater than that of the *aitu*.

The *aitu* of Malietoa was a fish called *anae*, a kind of mullet. On the appointed day the forbidden food was set before Malietoa. The incident created tremendous excitement. Friends and distant relatives had come from afar to witness the daring spectacle. Many expected all who ate to drop dead there and then. Those of the family who were to share the experiment were in some cases so frightened that they dosed themselves with oil and salt water as possible antidotes to the mana of the *aitu*. But Malietoa and a few others with him took no precautions. As a power encounter it had to succeed or fail on its own merits. By partaking as a social unit the encounter involved both Malietoa as an individual and his family as a group. They ate. The excitement subsided. No evil befell them. Thereafter for many the *aitu* was false. Malietoa's sons could endure the separation for no more than three weeks, and then pleaded for the family's permission to take the same step.

This incident led many people to dispense with their personal *aitu* or break taboos, and to put themselves under the instruction of the Christian teachers. The movement gained momentum. Chiefs took the initiative; and thus it was that when Williams arrived after twenty moons, he found villages all around the coast where large groups had eaten or desecrated their *aitu*, built chapels, and were awaiting the return of Williams with more teachers. Their gods had been discarded, evil spirits had been cast out, and the houses swept—and were empty (pp. 164–65).

More Than Superstition

Power encounters involve more than overcoming primitive superstitions; what is being encountered are powerful forces of evil, forces that enslave people in a variety of ways. C. Peter Wagner, writing in *Christian Life* magazine (February 1985) in an article entitled, "The Power Encounter," describes a power encounter involving demonic confrontation:

When Pak A [a church planter, a term for a missionary with the specific vocation of beginning/organizing new churches, in Central Sulawesi] entered a certain village to share the gospel, he found himself face to face with a powerful witch doctor known throughout the area. The witch doctor was determined to stop the spread of the gospel on the spot. With the village people looking on, he pointed his finger to a calendar that was hanging on a wall about ten feet away. Then he challenged Pak A.

"Watch the power of my gods," he cried, "then show me what your God can do!" With that the calendar was instantly torn apart.

Pak A was shocked. But . . . he tuned in to the miraculous power of God in signs and wonders. He opened his heart to the Holy Spirit, and received instructions directly from God. He spoke gently but firmly to the witch doctor and those gathered around.

"The evil spirits always tear things apart and destroy them," he declared. "But the good God came to correct them and help us."

With that he pointed his finger at the torn calendar and a miracle happened. Instantly the calendar was put back the way it originally was!

No wonder Pak A continued successfully to plant churches in Central Sulawesi.

Western Culture

Opposition to Christianity in Western culture takes on forms different from those found in non-Western cultures. This accounts for the decreased number of dramatic, overt power encounters in Western culture when compared with those in many non-Western cultures. In non-Western cultures, few people doubt the existence and power of evil spirits; and this awareness affects the way they live. They are able to *see* spiritual encounters as spiritual encounters, not look for a naturalistic explanation of the phenomena. In Western culture, many people deny the existence of evil spirits, and very few people feel their lives are affected in any way by them. In the West a spirit of skepticism and unbelief places a cloud of suspicion over *everything* supernatural—both good and evil.

In some instances power encounters in Western culture look quite similar to those in non-Western cultures—at least the initial encounter does. For example, in *Power Evangelism* we tell the story of Melinda, a young woman who manifested all the signs of demon possession. When John Wimber first encountered Melinda—he had been called late one night by a scared friend of hers—the demon said through Melinda, "You can't do anything with her. She's mine." Eventually the demon left Melinda, but not until after first putting up a fight. An event like this in a remote village in Africa would result in many members of a tribe converting to Christianity. In the United States it only raises questions about the relationship between mental illness and demonic delusions. This is not to say that this type of power encounter is never responsible for converting someone to Christianity in Western culture, only that it is not as effective in leading large groups of people to Christ. Most in our culture simply cannot accept the supernatural in any form.

Thus, most of the stories in this book involve the overcoming of unbelief concerning God's ability to act supernaturally in the world today. The means by which God accomplishes this in these authors vary, but all involve two factors: a growing awareness that something is missing in the Christian life, and a personal encounter with the Holy Spirit in which unbelief and skepticism are overcome.

KEVIN SPRINGER

Introduction

Throughout church history, personal testimonies—written and oral—have played a powerful role in revival and renewal movements. What greater drama can be found than the blinding and conversion of the persecutor Paul on the road to Damascus, from which he emerged a man who helped many to see Jesus? In the fourth century Augustine wrote his *Confessions,* a testimony of his conversion that remains widely read today. St. Thérèse of Lisieux's *The Story of a Soul* was a worldwide best-seller in the late nineteenth century; in it she describes her total submission to God's will in all things. Earlier in our century C. S. Lewis described his conversion in *Surprised by Joy*—a closely reasoned account of a search for God that is at once intensely intellectual yet, in the end, childlike. More recently, Charles Colson's testimony, *Born Again,* has been responsible for thousands of people becoming Christians.

All of these testimonies give honest accounts of the struggles and triumphs of real people. They point to particular aspects of the kingdom of God that every generation needs to know and experience. From Paul we learn that God's grace is sufficient to cover even the "chief of sinners." From Augustine we learn about the subtlety of sin and the vanity of seeking after God apart from Christ. St. Thérèse tells us about the simplicity of faith, while C. S. Lewis reassures us that intellectual honesty is not antithetical to Christianity. Charles Colson, the Watergate "hatchet man," illustrates that being born again really does mean becoming a new person, with new attitudes, desires, and abilities.

When Kevin Springer approached me about this book, I wondered what aspect of the kingdom of God *these* testimonies would highlight and how they would contribute to what God is doing in the world today. I believe they reflect much of what God is doing to prepare his church—especially evangelical Christians in Western civilization—for the challenges we will face in the latter part of the twentieth century. The chief challenge we face, I believe, is nothing less than *the maintenance and increase of a vital Christian witness in the midst of a civilization that is increasingly hostile to God.*

In this introduction I trace the development of some of the spiritual and intellectual forces in Western civilization that have reshaped the face of Christianity over the past three hundred years. My purpose in going back so far in Western history is to emphasize the enormity of the forces that Christians face today. After developing the larger picture, I make a few observations about how secularism in this century has affected evangelical Christians, drawing a few conclusions about what this means for our future.

The Enlightenment

In the Middle Ages, God was acknowledged as the controlling force of the universe, and all life experiences—good and evil—were passively accepted as expressions of God's will. But the world changed following the Renaissance and Reformation—there were the religious wars, the rise of modern nation-states, the scientific discoveries of Bacon, Galileo, and Newton, and the influence of Hume and Descartes in philosophy. Western culture spurned the Bible and the church, and with them spurned God as the final authority for all matters of life. God was dethroned, and the human mind was installed as the measure of all things. During this period, called the Enlightenment, men and women set themselves free from what they saw as the ignorance and prejudice of the Middle Ages.

By the nineteenth century, materialism and rationalism had become dominant forces in Western intellectual life. Materialism assumes that nothing exists except matter and its movement and modifications. For a materialist, only what can be seen, tested, and proved is real. Rationalism seeks a reasoned explanation for all experience, making the human mind its chief guide in all matters. When thought of this way, reason is king.

During the Enlightenment many people thought it was possible to analyze all experience rationally and to arrive at objective truth even in such areas as ethics; that is, they thought it was possible to derive moral values from rationalism. This type of thinking is still popular today. In May 1987 the Princeton Religion Research Center conducted a poll of Americans in which 43 percent of the respondents thought morals and ethics should be based on "human experiences over the centuries." Only 44 percent said they should be based on "religious values." Thirty-five percent of those identified as evangelicals and 48 percent of the nonevangelicals looked primarily to human experience to form morals and ethics.

It was only a matter of time before thinkers and philosophers adopted this approach and applied it to biblical studies. This approach to Scripture, called theological liberalism, reached its zenith in the late nineteenth and early twentieth century. Theologians and philosophers such as Albert Schweitzer (*The Quest of the Historical Jesus*), Immanuel Kant (*Critique of Pure Reason* and *Critique of Practical Reason*), Friedrich Schleiermacher (*Discourses on Religion*), and Ludwig Feuerbach (*The Essence of Christianity*) were key figures of theological liberalism. On the one hand, these men rejected the supernatural elements of the Bible as nonhistorical myths or merely as local tales that had been handed down over the centuries by naive prescientific people. On the other hand, they attempted to retain the moral teaching of the Bible. In their attempts to make the Bible "relevant" to modern men and women, liberal theologians replaced divine revelation with human reason or human experience as the ultimate source of authority.

Post-Enlightenment

By the twentieth century the face of the Enlightenment had been radically altered. In fact, writers like Francis Schaeffer and Lesslie Newbigin call the latter part of the twentieth century the "post-Enlightenment" period. The Enlightenment failed to deliver what it promised, because objective moral truth cannot be derived from human experience and human reason alone. As a result, most intellectuals gave up the quest of discovering objective moral truth and purpose for being.

The Enlightenment's failure contributed to the moral crisis in Western civilization that we see around us today. The cover of the May 25, 1987, issue of *Time* magazine asks, "What Ever Happened to Ethics?" "Assaulted by sleaze, scandals and hypocrisy, America searches for its moral bearings," it reports. *Time* is surprised by the lack of ethics in America (a problem common to all Western democracies, I might add). But without a theological or philosophical basis for ethics, how can there be agreement on what is good and evil, right and wrong? Relativism and selfism are the inevitable stepchildren of a society that replaces God with human reason.

Another consequence of the Enlightenment's failure is the rise of religious pluralism, which creates a hostile atmosphere for Christianity. Religious pluralism proposes there is no one true religion: all religions are said to have equal value. "You can believe anything you want," religious pluralists say, "so long as you are sincere. Just do your own thing with God." Within the context of pluralism, Christianity becomes just another religion.

The failure of the Enlightenment left the philosophy of modern science as the dominant philosophical influence in Western society in this century. Modern science, a natural extension of the Enlightenment, is also built on the values of materialism and rationalism. But unlike Enlightenment philosophy, modern science does not claim any authority over religious or ethical matters. Why? Because spiritual reality—angels and demons, heaven and hell, redemption and damnation—cannot be measured scientifically. Thus it has no scientific validity.

Lesslie Newbigin, in his book *Foolishness to the Greeks,* points out two consequences of this for religion. First, Western men and women live in a "public world" dominated by "what our culture calls facts, in distinction from the private world of beliefs, opinions, and values" (p. 14). In the public world—the world of mathematics and medicine, politics and sociology—through the inductive method of modern science (conclusions based on observation and reason) we arrive at true understanding of how and why things work. "The real world disclosed by the work of science was one governed not by purpose but by natural laws of cause and effect. . . . Nature—the sum total of what exists—is the really real. And the scientist is the priest who can unlock for us the secrets of nature and give us the practical mastery of its workings" (pp. 24-25).

Second, Newbigin points out, "this inductive method has a limited validity in that it cannot decide this question: By whom and for what purpose was this whole world created?" (p. 14). In practice this means that, regarding religion and ethics (a category Newbigin calls "values"), every individual is "free, within very wide limits, to adopt and hold his or her own views about what is good and desirable, about what kind of life is to be admired, about what code of ethics should govern one's private life. . . . Here the operative principle is pluralism, respect for the freedom of each person to choose the values that he or she will live by" (pp. 16-17).

Inconsistencies

While one is thus allowed to believe anything regarding religious or ethical values (indeed, religious pluralism *encourages* diversity of opinion), the public world frowns on pluralism in the realm of scientific matters, which are considered matters of "fact." So, for example, to challenge evolutionary theory is threatening not because it challenges the meaning of certain findings of geology and paleontology, but because it brings into question the whole philosophy of modern science. Creation scientists, who believe that the Genesis account of creation has scientific validity, root their theory in religion and thus, no matter what scientific facts they may muster in their favor, are considered scientific heretics. And, just as in the days of the Inquisition, there can be no public debate with heretics. Allan Bloom, in his best-selling book *The Closing of the American Mind,* writes, "The most successful tyranny is not the one that uses force to assure uniformity, but the one that removes the awareness of other possibilities, that makes it seem inconceivable that other ways are viable" (p. 249). That is what post-Enlightenment, scientific thought has done to religiously based alternative explanations of human origin. (My purpose in raising the issue of creationism versus evolutionism is only to illustrate the closed mind of America. Discussion surrounding the issue of creationism itself is a separate subject.)

We live in a strange age, for most modern men and women who claim to be rigorous rationalists are irrationalists when it comes to religion and morality. This partially explains the explosion of Eastern religions in the West in recent years: most Eastern religions appear to accept the value of religious pluralism. None claims to be the *only* way to God, only one of many ways.

Christianity, on the other hand, is exclusive: it claims there is no way to God except through Christ. Jesus said, "I am the way and the truth and the life. *No one comes to the Father except through me*" (John 14:6). This is a highly offensive statement to modern ears. It sounds so narrow, so bigoted, so . . . *fundamentalist.* And with the widening influence of post-Enlightenment thought it will become offensive to even more people as the century draws to a close.

Evangelical Response

These developments in Western culture have had a fragmenting effect in the church. Their influence in mainline Protestant churches (especially the seminaries) led to the ascendancy of liberal theology earlier in this century. Many Protestants believe that the influence of liberal theology is in part responsible for the loss of spiritual vitality and membership in many of these churches. (Over the last twenty-five years the Roman Catholic church has been going through a similar crisis.)

Much more could be said about the effects of the Enlightenment among mainline Protestants and Catholics, but this book is concerned with evangelicals. During the nineteenth century, some Christians— forerunners of modern evangelicals—resisted the more extreme influences of secular thinking; they refused to discard the supernatural when reading and interpreting Scripture. They stressed the New Testament doctrines of conversion, new birth, and justification by grace. They also stressed that the Bible is the inspired and only infallible, authoritative Word of God and that events like the resurrection and the healings by Jesus actually happened in space and time. This brought them into conflict with theological liberals within the denominations and with secularists outside the churches.

When Christians confronted theological liberals, such as in the fundamentalist-modernist controversies of the 1920s or the many battles for control of major seminaries, they lost. They lost for two reasons. First, the scholarship of the liberals was superior to that of the conservatives. They had taken the lead in New and Old Testament studies. (For example, it was the higher critical scholars who produced some of the best Greek and Hebrew lexicons and many of the critical commentaries. Many of these works are still widely used today by scholars of all persuasions.) Second, they lost in the popular media, which presented them as hopelessly outdated.

Even though they lost control of the seminaries and key institutions, the conservative Christians refused to give up the fight. Instead, they changed the front, reorganizing and building new institutions. Over the past fifty years evangelicals have built up new denominations, seminaries, and parachurch organizations that are as influential as their old liberal counterparts, most of whom have long since fallen on hard times.

Necessary but Inadequate

Today evangelical scholars have regained a measure of the academic respect and credibility that their forerunners—men like F. J. A. Hort, J. B. Lightfoot, and B. F. Westcott—had attained at the beginning of this century. This is especially true in the field of Old and New Testament studies. Evangelical scholars are continuing to use and develop many of the "scientific" methods of Bible study that before the fundamentalistic reaction of the 1930s and 1940s were employed by all, liberals and conservatives.

For example, evangelical scholars are using archaeology, form criticism, linguistics, and data from other disciplines to elucidate the meaning of biblical texts. The difference between the liberal's use of these disciplines and that of the evangelical lies in the area of presuppositions. The conservative believes that behind whatever literary phenomena the text may hold lies some aspect of God's self-disclosure. In using every critical tool at his or her disposal the evangelical's goal is to discern what the Scripture meant to its original audience so that we can better understand what God intends to say to us today through his Word.

Though the evangelicals who use these historical-critical methods hold to basic orthodoxy about the person and work of Christ, nevertheless some of them have yielded to Enlightenment thinking in some important ways. For example, many have discounted the supernatural for today. Signs and wonders were valid for the first century, they said, but are no longer needed today. I am aware that most conservative evangelicals offer theological rationales for their denial of the supernatural today, and I do not regard their arguments lightly. But I would also point out that their position on the supernatural today appears to smack of Enlightenment thought.

The historical-critical method itself is not responsible for this departure, though I believe at times it inclines Christians away from a deeper spirituality. Commenting on the historical-critical method in *The Use of the Bible in Theology—Evangelical Options,* New Testament scholar Russell P. Spittler says, "The historical-critical method when applied to Scripture, is both legitimate and necessary—but inadequate, . . . inadequate because . . . the end of biblical study cannot consist in historical dates or tentative judgments about complicated and conjectured literary origins. The end of biblical study consists rather in enhanced faith, hope and love both for the individual and the community" (p. 97). Reliance on this method of Scripture study, which dominates most Western conservative evangelical theological seminaries and graduate schools, can produce *intellectual,* but not necessarily *spiritual* Christian leaders.

I believe that downgrading the possibility for the supernatural today helps explain the legalism found in many conservative churches. The Bible is full of examples of men and women who allow external laws to replace heartfelt obedience to God's Word when they resist the Holy Spirit. I recently received a letter from a pastor from the Midwest who describes this frustration well:

Last fall I read your book on *Power Evangelism,* along with Martyn Lloyd Jones's book, *Joy Unspeakable.* As a result, the Spirit of God began to initiate a journey that is beginning to affect my preaching and ministry. For some time now, I have been dissatisfied with the church. Even though God has given me success in seeing a church grow (from 200 to 2000) in eight years, I am sick of seeing and working with people whose sole goal in life is learning "Bible knowledge"—which usually means learning facts from the Bible.

We saw close to 500 families become Christians, but within a few years something happened. Many developed lead bottoms and came to church with a "feed me" attitude. I began to see that I had to change what I was doing. I was killing the people with the Word! Isn't that something? They were suffering from the disease of "Scripturitis." That's what the Pharisees had, and Jesus spoke bluntly to them when he said, "You search the Scriptures, for in them you think you have eternal life. But you do not come to me that you might have life" (John 5:39).

This pastor is losing confidence in an approach to the Christian life that tends to limit spirituality to Scripture study. His crisis has come because this approach does not deliver what it promises.

Some people could infer that we must lay less stress on Scripture and replace it with a frenetic searching after signs and wonders and other irrational supernatural experiences. But this is not my point at all! Scripture, the Old and New Testaments, is God's Word to humans. It is without error and our guide in all areas of faith, morals, and practice. We receive faith as we hear the message of Christ (Rom. 10:17). The Word of God is powerful; it is "living and active . . . it judges the thoughts and attitudes of the heart" (Heb. 4:12).

My call is to place our confidence in Scripture *more firmly.* I believe this can happen only as we understand the purpose for which Scripture is given: to point us to a relationship with Jesus Christ. As long as the historical-critical method of Bible study supports and strengthens that relationship, it is legitimate. But when we forget the purpose and goal of our study, when the mere accumulation of information *about* God replaces a relationship *with* God, we run the risk of falling into legalism.

The Bible is analogous to a menu in a restaurant. We do not eat menus, we eat the meals that menus tell us about. Menus are of vital importance to restaurants, for without them we couldn't order our meals. Scripture functions in the same manner, telling us about the meal, the goal of our faith: Jesus Christ, Lord and Savior.

A common thread going through all of the testimonies in this book is each author's belief that the Bible is the Word of God. Because of this, these authors are not satisfied with merely studying about God; they want to know him and to be known fully by him.

Evangelicals in the Twentieth Century

In view of this historical background of the Enlightenment and nineteenth-century evangelicalism and liberalism, it is not difficult to understand why evangelicalism has undergone many changes during this century. In fact, evangelical Christians today are a diverse group that include conservatives, fundamentalists, Pentecostals, and charismatics. They are concentrated in their own denominations, but they are also heavily represented among mainline Protestants and Roman Catholics. There is much we can learn for the future by looking back on how and why these diverse groups came into being.

Pentecostals

I do not believe it is coincidence that modern Pentecostalism, what C. Peter Wagner calls the First Wave of the Holy Spirit, started around the turn of the century. With the collapse of the Enlightenment and the rise of post-Enlightenment thinking that allowed for nonrational, private religious experiences, the environment created a hunger in people for all kinds of personal religious experiences—good and bad. Modern theological liberalism offered little more than a code of ethics—something people could find just as easily outside of the church. And evangelicalism in the nineteenth century left many Christians with a hunger for more of an ongoing supernatural experience of God.

This is not to imply that Pentecostalism is irrational, only that it encourages a direct, personal relationship with the Holy Spirit that cannot always be understood in strict rationalist terms. So long as these experiences remained private matters, Pentecostalism was of little concern to the broader culture.

This was not the reaction of most evangelical Christians, though.

They bitterly opposed the Pentecostals, formally ostracizing them until 1943, when the National Association of Evangelicals offered membership to several Pentecostal denominations. (Even at that, serious cooperation between Pentecostals and the rest of evangelicalism did not occur until well into the 1970s.)

What is most remarkable about Pentecostalism is its phenomenal growth. By 1980 the Pentecostals (churches such as Assemblies of God, International Church of the Foursquare Gospel, Church of God in Christ, and Pentecostal Holiness Church) comprised the largest denominational subgroup among all Protestants worldwide, with over 51 million members. C. Peter Wagner believes that as of 1985 there were 85 million Pentecostals worldwide, if certain of the African independent churches are included. (The 1982 *World Christian Encyclopedia* estimates 345 million Protestants worldwide.) The greatest part of this growth has occurred in the latter half of the century.

Charismatics

The Second Wave of the Holy Spirit's work among evangelicals began in the early 1960s in the charismatic renewal, a renewing and reforming movement within mainline Protestant and Catholic churches in the West. Over the past twenty-five years the ranks of the charismatics have swollen to over 16 million Protestants and 35 million Catholics.

Whereas the First Wave seemed mainly to touch men and women from lower and lower-middle social and economic classes, the Second Wave was concentrated among middle-class mainline Protestants and Roman Catholics. The leaders of the charismatic renewal are formally educated and were raised in denominational churches. They generally remained within their denominations rather than moving out into independent style ministries, though this began to change in the late 1970s. They are usually pastors of or are closely tied in with congregations, though they may also travel extensively, conducting healing seminars and services. Their focus, even in their travels, is often primarily to members of their own denomination.

Because they tend to stay within their denomination, they do not appear as evangelistic as the Pentecostals. But this can be misleading, for many nominal members of Protestant and Catholic congregations experience a personal conversion to Jesus Christ through their ministries.

In recent years some members of the charismatic renewal have left their denominations to join Pentecostal churches or independent charismatic churches. This latter group, which in the United States has grown 557 percent in this decade, is by far the fastest expanding group in North America. (They are also probably the fastest growing churches in Great Britain.) A research assistant to C. Peter Wagner estimates there are at least 750,000 independent charismatics in the United States, and he said he wouldn't be surprised if there were actually twice that many.

Numbers That Cannot Be Ignored

C. Peter Wagner estimates that in 1985 there were 178 million Pentecostals and charismatics worldwide, with a decadal growth rate of 224 percent. "If accurate," he observes in an unpublished article for the *Dictionary of Pentecostal and Charismatic Movements* (to be published by Zondervan), "it represents what would undoubtedly prove to be one of the highest recorded rates of growth of a nonpolitical, nonmilitaristic human movement across history." (Wagner's estimate of 178 Pentecostals and charismatics worldwide pales in comparison to David B. Barrett's most recent estimate of 277 million worldwide. Barrett is a leading research missiologist and editor of the *World Christian Encyclopedia*.)

I have taken the space here to carefully lay out these numbers to make one point: the face of evangelicalism is changing, and it is changing quickly. Fundamentalists and conservative evangelicals who are noncharismatic no longer can afford to ignore the first two waves of the Holy Spirit in this century. They are surrounded.

One of these two groups, the fundamentalists, have insulated themselves from Pentecostals and charismatics. Most fundamentalists (though not all) stand outside of the first two great waves of the Holy Spirit, holding on to fifty-year-old criticisms of Pentecostal excesses. As the move of the Holy Spirit grows around them, I believe many of them could become more vocal in their opposition to Pentecostals and charismatics, while some will be anointed and transformed.

The second group, the conservative evangelicals, is already beginning to show signs of being the object of a new wave, the Third Wave, of the Holy Spirit's work in this century. By conservative evangelicals I mean a subgrouping within evangelicalism that is noncharismatic but not necessarily anticharismatic. This is a group of which I was a part for many years.

The Third Wave

C. Peter Wagner coined the term "Third Wave." Here is what he said about it in an article entitled "The Third Wave Goes Public" in the January 1986 issue of *Christian Life* magazine:

The term "Third Wave" has been with us for about three years. It seems to have caught on to a considerable degree. People now know we are not referring to Alvin Toffler's book of the same name, but to the third wave of the power of the Holy Spirit in the twentieth century. . . .

The Third Wave began around 1980 with the opening of an increasing number of traditional evangelical churches and institutions to the supernatural working of the Holy Spirit, even though they were not, nor did they wish to become, either Pentecostal or charismatic. . . .

One of the characteristics of the Third Wave is the absence of divisiveness. Many churches which do not have Pentecostal or charismatic backgrounds are beginning to pray for the sick and witness God's healing power while avoiding what some have considered (rightly and wrongly) the excesses of the past.

Dr. Wagner's last point, the absence of divisiveness, is what excites me most about the Third Wave. I am aware that there is some reaction among Christians to my books *Power Evangelism* and *Power Healing*. But my highest priority and the spirit in which I wrote them is for peace and unity in the body of Christ. The key to this unity is found in spiritual renewal, the type of renewal the contributors to this book describe. Donald G. Bloesch, in the second volume of *Essentials of Evangelical Theology,* writes, "The only genuine spiritual way to true . . . unity [among Christians] is a return to the message and teachings of Scripture with the aid of the tradition of the whole church. *Yet this return will involve not only an acceptance of right doctrine but also a renewal of personal faith. . . . The conversion that we call for is a spiritual as well as an intellectual one*" (p. 289, emphasis mine).

This book contains testimonies from men and women who are a part of the Third Wave and who have been touched in some way by my ministry. They represent a wide variety of Christian traditions—Protestant and Catholic. They come from a variety of ministries—pastors, evangelists, missionaries, teachers, professors—and from different parts of the world—the United States, Canada, Britain, and New Zealand. They attended renewal meetings for a variety of reasons—some were talked into coming, others came for the warm California weather, and a few were dragged along. None was prepared for what he or she saw and heard.

But there are some common elements in all of their stories:

- Almost all of them would identify themselves as evangelicals.
- They recognized a large gap between what they had been taught about God and their experience.
- They recognized in our ministry a way to bridge that gap.
- They held suspicions that needed to be allayed and they asked questions that needed answering before they could move ahead in their experience with the Holy Spirit.
- They all had an encounter with God, dramatic in most instances, that caught them by surprise. Most wanted information and help for ministry, and what they received was a changed life!

A good analogy for what happened to them is what happens to those who venture too close to a lion's cage. They run the risk of being eaten up by something more powerful than themselves.

Agents of Change

The Pentecostal and charismatic movements are only two of the forces reshaping evangelicalism. Other forces are heightened awarenesses of such social concerns as racism, protection of the unborn, and care for the hungry and homeless. These concerns are compelling many evangelicals to venture out from their churches and onto the streets. Finally, the necessity of defending the integrity of Scripture against attack is reminding them that Scripture is the word of God and must be obeyed.

Still, it is the challenges of living in a secular age, an age that is attempting to muzzle the church through pluralism and the privatization of all religious experience, that is the most potent force working against Christians today. The darkness is getting darker, but some people—among them the people in this book—are being prepared to shine like the noon-day sun.

The Acts 4 Syndrome

Our time is not too dissimilar to Peter and John's day. They too lived in a pluralistic society that wanted to stifle the proclamation and demonstration of the kingdom of God. Acts 4 is the story of their arrest for preaching the resurrection of Jesus. When dragged before the Sanhedrin (the "rulers, elders and teachers of the law"), Peter proclaimed, "Salvation is found in no one else [referring to Jesus], for there is no other name under heaven given to men by which we must be saved" (v. 12).

The religious leaders' response, so much like the response of modern men and women, was to "warn these men to speak no longer to anyone in this name" (v. 17). Peter and John did not hesitate before saying, "Judge for yourselves whether it is right in God's sight to obey you rather than God. For we cannot help speaking about what we have seen and heard" (vv. 19–20).

On their release Peter and John gathered the church and prayed, "Stretch out your hand to heal and perform miraculous signs and wonders through the name of your holy servant Jesus" (v. 30). God immediately answered their prayers: "After they prayed, the place where they were meeting was shaken. And they were all filled with the Holy Spirit and spoke the word of God boldly" (v. 31).

All of the people in this book have stood in a place that was shaken and then been filled with the Holy Spirit. And the reason for that shaking and filling is the same today as it was in the first century: that they might speak the word of God boldly.

JOHN WIMBER

I

Personal Encounters

Sometimes God does not use a specific occasion or crisis to bring about a power encounter—he simply sends his Holy Spirit. In fact, many people feel quite good about their lives at the time of their power encounters. All three people in this section perceived no great needs in their lives; they thought they were doing well, that they were on the crest of the wave of what God was doing in the world. But then the Holy Spirit came on them, and they discovered that for some time they had been floating dead in the ocean.

1

A Hunger for God

Carol Wimber

Carol Wimber, John Wimber's wife, was instrumental in the founding of the Vineyard Christian Fellowship of Anaheim, California.

Shortly after John resigned as pastor of our local church, Yorba Linda Friends Church, in 1974, I noticed changes in it that were unsettling to me. As an elder, teacher, and board member, I was in a good position to observe congregational trends. I noticed the weaker members were leaving the church and church growth waned. I had to admit that our church, which stood for all we believed in and which we were so proud of, was slipping away.

My first reaction to declining attendance was to try harder to maintain growth. I taught more Bible studies and Sunday school classes. I helped develop new and more effective Vacation Bible School programs. I gave it all I had.

By 1976 I was teaching women's Bible studies around Orange County and I was beginning to feel confident about myself, though I was still disturbed about our local congregation. "Lord," I would ask in my prayers, "what's wrong with the church? Why are so many people wandering away now that John is no longer pastor?" I wasn't prepared for how God would answer my prayers.

A Disturbing Dream

I might have gone on in that flourish of activity if it hadn't been for a disturbing dream I had in September of 1976. In the dream I was standing on a soap box at the end of my street preaching to a large crowd against the gifts of the Holy Spirit. I considered myself an expert on the subject. After all, for years I had been responsible for running off members of the church who practiced gifts like tongues, healing, or prophecy—gifts I considered dangerous and divisive. I was preaching through my well-rehearsed seven-point sermon when, at the final point, a sensation like hot electricity hit my head, traveled down my body, then went up again and out of my mouth. I awakened speaking in tongues.

I was so troubled by the dream and experience of speaking in tongues that, like a bag of sand with a hole in it, my confidence and self-assurance trickled away. "Perhaps," I thought, "I don't know as much as I thought I did about the Christian life. Maybe I have been a Pharisee all of these years." What frightened me so much was that I thought I had been sincere with God. I judged everyone else's relationship with God according to my personal standards—the closer they came to believing and behaving as I did, I thought, the closer they were to God. That is a pitiful confession, but that is the way I lived.

I had gone to God asking him what was wrong with the church, and he was showing me what was wrong with me. And he wasn't finished with me yet.

The pressure of these thoughts built up, culminating a few weeks later in my falling on my bed in tears. "Oh God," I cried out, "if all that stuff [meaning spiritual gifts like tongues and healing] is from you, than I have barely known you all these years." There was a long silence. Than I sensed in my heart a gentle answer: "You're right."

I was so devastated that I stopped teaching, resigned from the church board, and stopped giving my opinion about anything spiritual. I abandoned all that I had been devoted to for so long and hid out at home for three weeks, weeping and repenting of my attitude toward God and his Spirit. Today I look back on that experience as a "personality meltdown," a breaking of my self-will that was so profound I have never been the same since.

During this time God showed me how blind and naked I was, how in my self-assurance I had missed knowing him for years. Then he showed me what he had meant to do through John years before and how I had stood in the way and prevented John from moving out in greater faith and power.

My heart was broken. My tears were pleas for mercy as he showed me all that I had been responsible for John missing. Fifteen years before, shortly after we were converted, John spoke in tongues and prayed for our son's healing, and I persuaded him that it was not from God. The turning away from those experiences wounded John, saddling him with a sense of loss that he had not recovered from. God had a pattern, a blueprint for renewal, and John was a key in what God wanted to do. But so far we had missed it, and I was responsible.

While I cried I prayed over and over again the only prayer of mercy I knew, the old Catholic Latin Gregorian chant, "Kyrie Eleison, Christi Eleison; Lord have mercy, Christ have mercy." Nothing else mattered. For three weeks I slept little and couldn't eat.

Hunger for God

Out of this terrible crucible of guilt and sorrow a desperate longing and hunger for God emerged. This hunger was not for his will, it was for God himself. Psalm 73:21–22 became my passage: "When my heart was grieved and my spirit embittered, I was senseless and ignorant; I was a brute beast before you." I knew that I had come from pride and arrogance to senselessness and ignorance. In verse 25 the Psalm goes on to say, "Whom have I in heaven but you? And being with you, I desire nothing on earth." That verse described my passion for God. I've never been interested in anything else since then.

This was happening to me during a time when God was also speaking to John. He had been working for two years at the Charles E.

Fuller Institute of Evangelism and Church Growth but was sensing God calling him back into the pastorate. Little did I know that the Holy Spirit was orchestrating change in both our lives simultaneously. The Holy Spirit had not forsaken us; he would restore those lost years.

John's preoccupation with God's dealings in his own life worked to my advantage during this time. Once John came home from a business trip (he was traveling frequently), saw my red puffy eyes, and asked what was wrong. "Me," I answered. "I'm wrong. I've been so wrong." He didn't know how to respond to me, so he enquired no further at that time about my condition.

In the middle of my pain I somehow felt that what was happening wasn't just for me and John, it was for all the people we had cared for over the years. So many had come to God only to later wander away. They experienced too little power, too little life. I saw our people wandering aimlessly, hungry for God. I had been responsible for encouraging Laodician thinking—thinking we were rich and in need of nothing when in fact we were wretched, miserable, poor, naked, and blind. They wanted more; they wanted to experience the living God of the Bible. God told me to make restitution with those people I had wounded. I went to many of the people I had driven out of the church and asked their forgiveness. They responded first with surprise and then with joy. As I was reconciled with those I had sinned against, God lifted the weight of my guilt. My tears began to dry.

Soon God stopped showing me what he had wanted to do in the past and began to show me what he was going to do in the future. I had a strong sense of God's desire for his bride, for the whole church—Protestant, Catholic, Orthodox.

"This Is It"

God used an unusual experience to tell me that what he had in store went beyond our little Quaker church. One afternoon I was sitting by our swimming pool and in my mind's eye I saw us all being baptized in the water. I was startled both by the vision itself and by the idea of water baptism; you see, Quakers do not practice water baptism. So from that moment I knew he was going to do something that went outside of our denominational boundaries.

All of this was still difficult for me to accept. I could see that we were haughty and unbelieving, desperately in need of change. And God promised that he would change us. But the change was not so much a revival as a transformation. It would be like getting caught up in the river described in Ezekiel 47—the water was too wide and deep for anyone to cross. Ezekiel said the river had a life of its own, sweeping away anyone who entered it. God was about to sweep us into his plans, and his plans had room for many, many people.

I told John very little about my experience, because my earlier influence in his life had been destructive. "Lord," I prayed, "if this is of you, then you influence John. I no longer trust myself in these matters."

Several months later God gave me liberty to tell John that if he, John, returned to the pastorate I would support him. (This was important because several years earlier I told him I never wanted to be a pastor's wife again.) I told him this in a restaurant after we attended a home prayer meeting that I helped lead. John had attended that evening for the first time and he was not impressed; all we did was pray and worship. After I told him I was willing to support him in returning to the pastorate he looked at me and said, "I suppose next you're going to tell me that you speak in tongues."

"Yep," I said. He almost drove his fork through the side of his mouth, because he knew that for me to speak in tongues meant God could do anything.

The home meeting we attended was started in October of 1976 by a few leaders in our church to encourage one another in their teaching ministries. When I heard about the gathering God said, "This is it," by which he meant this was the beginning of the church he had shown me. When I first attended I knew why. God was undoing the self-sufficiency of the leaders; they were becoming learners again—

students with a hunger for God. We would meet and break into small groups and pray for each other. We worshiped God for hours, content to sing and listen to his voice in our midst.

The meeting size grew from twelve to fifty in a few weeks. People who had been away from the church for years were coming back. Others were coming from everywhere, not even knowing why they were drawn to the meeting, for they had really heard very little about it. We would receive telephone calls from people around the country who were hungry for God.

People continued to come, mostly young people, until we were sitting knee to back on the floor throughout the entire house. John began attending fairly regularly in January of 1977. By March of 1977 there were over 125 adults attending, packing every room and hall, even spilling over onto the patio.

Healing

Eventually our denomination asked our group to leave, and we understood why they had to ask. They'd been good to us, and we hated leaving. We agreed to leave, but only under one condition: that the church write a letter of release and give their blessing. They did write the letter, encouraging us to do what God had called us to. With that we received an important spiritual blessing. In retrospect, I believe their blessing explains some of the shaking and quaking and signs and wonders that we later experienced. The history of the Friends of Jesus—or Quakers (as they were mockingly called by others)—was full of stories of the miraculous intervention of God. Leaving the church was difficult. After all, these people had been very kind to us over the years. We raised our children together, and many of them were our mentors. But God was calling us on to something new.

It was Mother's Day (May 8, 1977), the following week, that 150 people met for the first time as a new church that would later be named Vineyard Christian Fellowship. John was our pastor, and he preached that Sunday on the reputation of illegitimacy that followed

Jesus his whole life and how we, as a church born of the Spirit, would carry that stigma also. After he preached we worshiped for an hour and closed the meeting with prayer for each other.

Immediately after we became a church, John called a meeting of all the adults. He thought that for a church to grow in quantity and quality it must divide and form small groups. This was done to avoid the division between the "inner circle" of older members and the "outer circle" of newer members. We formed kinship groups, small units in which we could care for one another and meet needs. At first these groups were difficult, because we missed many of our old friends. But soon we discovered a deeper level of relationship with each other, and new members were being added.

John's attitude toward God, the church, and Scripture was quite different from what it had been in the past. Time and again he said that for years he had tried to run the church, but now he was committed to giving it to Jesus, no matter what the cost. John challenged us to read Scripture as learners and doers, never being content with only learning something new, but always aiming at changing the way we lived.

We read Scripture with new eyes. We could see clearly that Jesus and the early church healed the sick. We knew we had no idea about how we could heal the sick, but we wanted to learn how. John started teaching about healing, and we prayed for healing. Nothing happened; we became disillusioned. But we refused to give up. So some of us gathered in small groups and cried out to God, weeping and pleading for him to do what he promised in his word.

As is well known from John's writings, this went on for ten months, culminating in the healing of a woman with the flu after John prayed for her in February of 1978. During this period we were aware that the power we felt God had for us was missing. So we continued to pray and ask God what was wrong with us, what was missing in our lives, why we lacked power for healing. "Oh that you would rend the heavens," we would pray from Isaiah 64. "That you would come down! That the mountains might shake at your presence!"

Anointed for Ministry

In early April of 1978 more signs of spiritual renewal began to appear. Around this time John started teaching a home Bible study. One evening he taught on the baptism and filling of the Holy Spirit. Afterward someone said, "Well, why don't you pray for us now to be filled with the Holy Spirit?" So John went around the room praying for us, and an incredible power was released from his hands. He touched people and they fell over. To John it was as though spiritual power came from his hands like electricity. This was the first time John actually *felt* power coming through him in this way.

We were not Pentecostals. In fact, we had never seen or experienced anything like this. There was no way we could have been preprogrammed to fall over. Nor can I imagine *why* we would have wanted to fall over! So we could not deny the reality of the presence of God.

The following week John was once again teaching on healing. His text that day was about healing of the invalid (John 5:1–15). In attendance was a young girl who suffered from a childhood accident that caused decelerated growth in one of her legs. This created painful back problems for her. During the Bible study she went up and asked John if he would pray for her, specifically to cause her shortened leg to grow. At the end of the study he announced the girl's request, inviting her to sit in the center of the group and receive prayer. John had her sit down and began praying. When he placed his hand on her leg power was released; her leg began jerking and quivering. When she stood up everyone could see that one pants leg was shorter than the other. She was healed!

On the way home from this meeting John and I discussed the relationship between teaching something and then modeling it for a group of people. Instead of show and tell this was a method of tell and show. We walked into our home talking about this new discovery, and John went to the refrigerator to get a glass of milk. As he was pouring the milk, John said, "It must be that when you teach the word of God the Holy Spirit . . ."

He never finished his sentence. As he started to say "Holy Spirit" his legs buckled and he caught himself on the counter, splashing milk all over in the process. He looked up at me with a surprised grin and said, "I think we're on to something here, Carol Kay."

Soon John began receiving words of knowledge, the gift of the Spirit in which one receives specific information about a person or persons. He would stand before a group and see cones of light shining down on some people, those whom God was touching with his healing and renewing power. Before long the home Bible study was overflowing with people, some of whom were hungry to see miracles. We were afraid that many of them flocked to us only to get an experience, a spiritual "high." This grieved us deeply. During this time John considered stopping ministry in the Holy Spirit, because of the selfish motivation on the part of many who came, and because he never wanted to be a "big man" in ministry. God had already told him that this was to be the people's ministry. The church, John felt, had been kept exclusively in the hands of the clergy for too long.

John was struggling with how he could help others experience the power and presence of God that he was beginning to experience. We hadn't fully realized yet that through the laying on of hands one can give away what God gives. We had read that Moses and Elijah did it, but we didn't relate that to our experience. Then God spoke to John about anointing the people for ministry. One Sunday morning toward the end of the meeting, John called forward people who wanted greater power for ministry, had them take off their shoes, anointed them with oil according to Leviticus 8—on the right ear, the thumb of the right hand, and the big toe of the right foot. (This was the way Moses consecrated Aaron and his sons for ministry.) John also laid hands on them to release the spiritual gift of healing. He wasn't completely sure of himself at first, but he was sure that God told him to do it. After that he called for the sick to come forward and be prayed over by the people he had just anointed and prayed for. The results were staggering—many were healed.

So the congregation moved out into power healing, healing through the Holy Spirit. Soon many visitors were coming to see what we were doing. Sometimes we resented the way people came to watch us. But one morning a prophecy came that gave us peace: "*I've made you a marketplace.*" People were no longer apprehensive of us, because when we prayed for people we did it in a relaxed and gentle way. Our Quaker background made us more disposed to be quiet. There was no shouting or other loud behavior.

Come, Holy Spirit

On Mother's Day of 1981 we had a watershed experience that launched us into what today is called power evangelism. At this time John invited a young man who had been attending our church to preach on a Sunday evening. The young man shared his testimony, which was beautiful and stirring, then asked for all the people under the age of twenty-five (two-thirds of the congregation, which now numbered over seven hundred) to come forward. None of us had a clue as to what was going to happen next. When they got to the front the speaker said, "For years now the Holy Spirit has been grieved by the church, but he's getting over it. Come Holy Spirit."

And he came.

Most of these young people had grown up around our home and we knew them well—we had four children between the ages of eighteen and twenty-four. One fellow, Tim, started bouncing. His arms flung out and he fell over, but one of his hands accidentally hit a mike stand and he took it down with him. He was tangled up in the cord with the mike next to his mouth. Then he began speaking in tongues, so the sound went throughout the gymnasium (by now we were meeting in a high school). We had never considered ourselves charismatics and certainly had never placed emphasis on the gift of tongues. We had seen a few people tremble and fall over before and we had seen many healings, but this was different. The majority of the young people were shaking and falling over. At one point it looked like a battlefield scene—bodies everywhere, people weeping, wailing, and speaking in tongues, much shouting and loud behavior. And there was Tim in the middle of it all, babbling into the microphone.

A wide-eyed John sat by softly playing the piano. Some members of our staff were fearful and angry. Several people got up and walked out, never to be seen again—at least they were not seen by us.

But I knew that God was visiting us. I was so thrilled, because I had been praying for power for so long. This might not have been the way I wanted to see it come, but this was how God gave it to us. I got up and started stepping over bodies and putting my hand next to them. I could feel the power, like heat or electricity, radiating off of their bodies.

I asked one boy who was on the floor, "What's happening to you right now?" He said, "It's like electricity. I can't move!" I was amazed by the effect of God's power on the human body. I suppose I thought that it would all be an inward work, such as conviction or repentance. I never imagined there would be strong physical manifestations.

But John wasn't as happy as I. He had never seen large numbers of people sprawled out over the floor, yelling in tongues and shaking violently. He spent that night reading Scripture and historical accounts of revival from the lives of people like Whitefield and Wesley. He was afraid of doing anything that wasn't explicitly outlined in the Bible. But his study did not yield conclusive answers to questions raised from the previous evening's events. By 5 AM John was desperate. He cried out to God, "Lord, if this is you, please tell me." A moment later the phone rang and a pastor friend of ours from Denver, Colorado, was on the line. "John," he said, "I'm sorry I'm calling so early, but I have something really strange to tell you. I don't know what it means, but God wants me to say, 'It's me, John.' "

Power Encounters

That was all John needed. He didn't have to understand the trembling or why everything happened as it did; all he needed to know was Holy Spirit did it.

We met with our staff that morning, and the Holy Spirit came and healed old wounds and hurts, delivering us from fear. John declared that he was willing to put up with the discomfort of not knowing or understanding how the Holy Spirit works; never again, to the best of his ability, would he quench the Spirit.

At that time a revival broke out among our junior-high and high-school-aged young people. Hundreds of teenagers were converted to Christ through power encounters. Our young people witnessed to and healed others in the streets, restaurants, and stores. We baptized hundreds of new converts during the next few months, in our pool and in pools all around town.

John was cautious not to draw conclusions too quickly about what God was doing. Instead, he watched and prayed, asking God to bless what he was doing. We wanted what God wanted, not what we thought should happen. We learned to accept what God was doing, no matter how strange it appeared to us. We had to risk our reputation for the sake of knowing God.

The Lord has blessed the Anaheim Vineyard Christian Fellowship. We now have over five thousand members and have grown to over two hundred congregations in North America. But in the end all of this means nothing if that vital ingredient is missing: hunger for God.

2

The Third Wave Has Only Just Begun

Anne Watson

Anne Watson is executive officer of the Belfrey Trust, York, England. At St. Michael-le-Belfrey Anglican Church she serves as elder in charge of ministry and spiritual gifts and also oversees the banner, dance, and drama groups. She and her late husband, Canon David Watson, have two children.

My introduction to what has now become known as the Third Wave of God's Spirit occurred in 1980. My late husband, David Watson, a well-known English evangelist who was deeply concerned with renewal and reconciliation in the church, had just returned from one of his annual visits to Fuller Theological Seminary in Pasadena, California. He conducted seminars on evangelism and the renewal of the church for the Doctor of Ministry and Master of Divinity courses. He always found his time at Fuller stimulating, but this time I could see that something new had happened and it was obviously very important. He was so excited as he proceeded to tell me about the amazing church he had visited and its pastor, John Wimber. David had agreed to visit the church only after some persuasion, as his schedule at Fuller was always packed and there was little time for anything else.

I was apprehensive as he told me about this new friend he had made and all that he had seen in the Vineyard church. I wasn't sure where all this would lead, and I was jealous too. David could see that this news was getting a rather cool reception.

I was surprised and confused by my reactions. I had prayed for years that David would find someone with as "famous" a ministry as he had who would not "worship" him but be a real friend. David Watson was a household name in Great Britain through his city missions and many books, but that led to isolation and loneliness. All through our marriage I was the one who took the lead in the ministry of spiritual gifts, especially prophecy. David did not seem to get excited when I introduced some new area of the life of God—rather the reverse. There was always a lot of caution and I had to learn how to persuade him! But here he was enthusing about someone he had met only very briefly who was allowing all sorts of extraordinary things to happen in his church, and David thought it was marvelous.

An American in York

David invited John and his wife, Carol, to York, and they came with a team. I played it "cool" at first—more like an iceberg! How carnal we can be. God was working in dramatic ways. I was totally out of my depth, which surprised me as I thought I had a large capacity for entering into the new things the Spirit was doing. After all, hadn't I pioneered the way for the gifts of the Spirit in our church? And what a costly business that had been! At one point, I remember sitting in the pew at the beginning of a service and praying, "Oh Lord, I don't know if I like all this. It's so untidy and rather frightening and it might disrupt all that is going on at St. Michael's." The Lord answered, "Well, Anne, *I* like it. I am in charge of St. Michael's and I will work in the way I want to." I asked for forgiveness and help for my constricted attitudes. I realized how close I had come to quenching the Holy Spirit.

Negative reactions often precede the movement of God's Spirit. The Scriptures are full of such incidences. Moses did not want to go and confront Pharaoh, but subsequent events demonstrated the power of God dramatically. Gideon was very skeptical and fearful when God called him and it took two miracles to persuade him to agree. Even the Virgin Mary had questions when the Angel Gabriel announced that she would conceive a son miraculously. Peter asked Jesus to go away and leave him alone when he found himself unwillingly involved in a miracle. The disciples were clearly anxious when it came to feeding five thousand people with five loaves and two small fish! The Pharisees, when faced with the power of God in the life and ministry of Jesus, let tradition and self-interest become weapons against the Spirit. God is not averse to human reactions, but in the end we need to acknowledge his sovereignty.

Conversion

I had known the sovereignty of God when I first surrendered my life to Christ. I was training to be a nurse at Guy's Hospital in London and had made friends with some other nurses and doctors in the hospital who went to Christian meetings. Over coffee one evening we had a friendly argument about whether dogs went to heaven! I was advised to read John 3:16 by one of the young men. He was rather attractive so I read it—more to please him than anything else.

Back in my room I read the verse: "For God so loved the world that he gave his one and only Son, that whoever believes in him shall not perish but have eternal life." I was shattered. I realized that I had never thanked Jesus for dying to save my life. It had always been a rule in our family that when we received a gift we had to write a thank-you letter within three days. I had not said thank you to Jesus for twenty-one years! I dropped to my knees and asked Jesus to forgive me for being so late in thanking him. I then "opened the door of my heart" and asked him to come in as I had read in John 3:16. Suddenly Jesus was standing right beside me in a wonderful glowing light. I wasn't frightened, just tremendously happy. We just looked at each other and he smiled. He seemed to accept me so totally that it was as if I had known him all my life. I loved him from that moment. When he had gone I got into bed and fell asleep.

The next morning I woke and reached for my Bible and study notes, as was my habit. I was thunderstruck to find that it seemed so different. It was as if I had been struggling to read the Scriptures in a language I only understood in part—but now I could read it fluently and understand it easily. This convinced me that the experience of the previous evening had not been a figment of my imagination.

Dreams and Visions

A year later during midwifery training I had another dramatic encounter with God. It was during Lent and my discipline for that season was to be more abstemious about television viewing. I also decided it would be good to give some of my earnings to a charity. I saw an advertisement for needy children in a missionary home in Korea and sent a donation. A letter of thanks arrived from the British director along with an article by him entitled "With God Nothing Is Impossible—Or with You."

The article was based on two verses of Scripture: "If you have faith as a grain of mustard seed, you can say to this mountain, 'move' and it will" and "without faith it is impossible to please God." Being a practical person I thought I should conduct an experiment to measure my faith, as I wanted to be one of those who pleased God. There was no mountain in sight but a very large tree outside my window made a good substitute.

I had no doubt at all from reading the Bible that God was capable of doing the impossible. I looked at the tree and knew from what I had just read that if I had a little faith (after all a mustard seed is only very tiny), all I had to do was to say to the tree "move over the lawn" and it would move. I looked at the tree but realized very quickly that I certainly did not believe a command from me would make it move. My faith was nonexistent; I did not qualify to please God. I got down on my knees and prayed for forgiveness for my lack of faith and asked God to give me a gift of faith so that I could please him.

Then the most extraordinary thing happened. I was surrounded by a very white light and seemed to be rising up and up, and as I did so the light got more and more dazzling and I was frightened that any moment I would be in the presence of God. I said, "Put me down, please." Then I "woke" and heard someone talking, but I could not understand the language. I was about to ask them to speak in English when I realized with a shock that there was no one in the room except me. I was the one who was talking. I stopped immediately. What could this mean? I decided to go see if I could speak in this strange language at will and what would happen if I did. I opened my mouth and spoke—the language was still with me. I spoke hesitantly at first, but as I gained confidence the words seemed to form sentences. I could stop and start whenever I pleased. But the most wonderful thing that happened when I spoke in this language was that the presence of Jesus was overwhelming—I could have reached out and touched him.

I kept my experience secret for many weeks, as I thought my friends would think I was in need of psychiatric treatment. During Confirmation classes I was given a booklet that explained that this strange language was referred to by St. Paul in 1 Corinthians 14 and in other places in the Bible as speaking in tongues and was one of the gifts of the Spirit.

I realized, too, that God had not given me a greater measure of faith—he had given me an understanding that he was my Father. I had come into a family relationship with him. How much easier it was to ask him to do wonderful things and believe that he would. I entered a whole new dimension of living.

Prophecy

While sitting under the hair dryer one day I read in 1 Corinthians 14 that those who spoke in tongues should pray for the gift of interpretation. So I said to the Lord, "I'll speak in tongues, and please would you interpret it for me?" After speaking for a short time I waited and then, clear as a bell, words in English came into my head. Well, that wasn't too difficult. I practiced a few times, which helped when it came to interpreting in a church meeting.

Prophecy came after I began to understand that the church was the body of Christ. When I asked God to show me what the body of his Son looked like in our church, he used the story of the good

Samaritan. Jesus in St. Cuthbert's (we later moved to St. Michael's) was beaten and wounded rather like the man who had fallen among thieves. It was heartbreaking. I took note that the Samaritan had used oil to heal the wounds. Taking oil as a symbol of the Holy Spirit, I looked to see if any of the gifts of the Spirit were particularly applicable. I read in 1 Corinthians 14 that prophecy edifies the church. I asked God earnestly for this gift as I wanted to see the body of Jesus restored. I found that instead of getting the interpretation of a tongue in a meeting, I found English words coming into my head *before* there was a message in tongues. Only the first few words of the sentence were given. If I gave them out would any others follow? The only way to find out was to speak them out. Follow they did and this gift has been one of the major ways God has called me to minister in his body in York.

However, when the "Third Wave" began to break over my head, nothing that had gone before seemed to be of any help except for one thing—God was my Father and I knew his voice. He had told me he liked all the things that were happening when John and his team ministered to us in York, so I decided I should be better acquainted with them too! I came to all the meetings after that. But my frustrations increased, especially when I couldn't see the Spirit on people. I stared sometimes until my eyes were popping out of my head! However, I was excited by what I did see when John and the team were ministering and I helped many people get over their initial fears.

Most of the excitement and manifestations died down after our visitors returned to the States and we carried on as before. Well, nearly: I prayed for a few sick people during Holy Communion but since none of them got better I decided I would stick to prophesying. That at least brought results.

David's Crisis

In June 1984 we moved to London, partly to facilitate David's traveling ministry and partly to allow St. Michael's to grow and develop in new ways under the man God had called for that purpose. In

January during a routine visit to his doctor, David was found to have cancer of the colon. This was treated successfully by surgery, but a secondary growth was found in the liver. He had only a year to live. I felt totally inadequate and unprepared. It seemed so unfair that my first "case" of real illness should be my own husband with a terminal disease. I felt I was facing an enemy armed only with a bow and arrow, when what I really needed was an exocet missile. The story of David's last year is well documented in his book *Fear No Evil,* and John Wimber also comments on it in *Power Healing.*

We spent ten hilarious days with John and Carol Wimber in California after David had recovered from surgery. I was still struggling with the Spirit. The first time I entered the gymnasium where the Vineyard meetings were held I started to shake—and the service hadn't even started. I sat down on one of the chairs and hung on to the edge as tightly as possible. God seemed to have no sensitivity to my feelings!

However, when the worship started I felt thoroughly at home even though tears kept streaming down my cheeks. When people were asked to go for prayer in the adjoining room, David was up from his seat like a shot—not to be ministered to but to pray for others. He seemed to be enjoying every minute of it. I wished I were a thousand miles away. However, I decided the most inconspicuous thing to do was to join one of the praying groups. That was not as easy as it looked. Everyone seemed to know what they were doing and I felt rather embarrassed peering in. Not very polite! Then I saw one of the pastors I knew, and he called me over. He was interviewing a woman who was having difficulty sleeping. He asked her to look at him and suddenly her eyes seemed to go up into the top of her head leaving only the whites showing. My first reaction was "Help! This is a demon." My second reaction was to look for an exit sign. There was one right beside us! I felt reassured that the Lord did understand. I braced myself—for I don't know what—only to find that the pastor asked the woman to close her eyes and he prayed the Lord's peace upon her. Then he asked her to make an appointment to come to the office for more prayer during the week. She agreed, smiled, and left. I was dumbstruck. Fancy leaving that poor woman with a demon if that was what it was. Swallowing my anger and plucking up courage, I asked him, "Did she have a demon?"

"Yes," he replied.

"Why didn't you cast it out?"

"She has had it for quite a number of years and I am very tired tonight. It's best left until we can deal with it effectively during the day."

It all seemed so undramatic and sensible. I was learning.

One afternoon John switched on the TV so we could watch a man ministering to the sick. We saw some children healed from deafness and I found myself crying and crying and crying. David was embarrassed but John just sat and smiled. I was so angry with John. Why didn't he do something about my condition? After all he was supposed to know about this sort of thing. My embarrassment increased when the doorbell rang and Carol had to deal with two Jehovah's Witnesses who could see all that was going on. When they left she came over and John said, "The Holy Spirit is on Anne." She smiled and said, "I'll make a cup of tea." I know the English are supposed to like tea a lot, but this hardly seemed the moment! It was a practical lesson about the sovereignty of God. When he chooses to send the Spirit on us, our ideas of appropriateness need to take second place. John and Carol's example of accepting the supernatural as a part of everyday living was an eye-opener.

There were other times, too, when it seemed "inappropriate" for the Spirit to manifest himself. This usually happened in parking lots, although he must have taken note of my feelings because it always happened when it was dark! I would be leaving a restaurant with David, John, Carol, and others when my hands would start to shake and John would grab them and lay them on David saying it was a pity to waste all that power. This could go on for quite a while and turn into a time of praying for quite a lot of people.

David and I returned to London refreshed and encouraged. After a number of months of freedom from symptoms David's condition deteriorated and he visited the Vineyard in Anaheim again. Teams prayed for him around the clock but to no avail. He came home. The battle that raged got fiercer and fiercer until early on a February morning David went to be with the Lord.

Anointing for Ministry

In July I returned to York and I made a vow to God that whatever it cost, I wanted to learn to pray for the sick. To do this I have attended the signs and wonders conferences held in England and gradually the panic that rose with the mention of the words "healing clinic time" have subsided! Now I look forward to it with anticipation. I had lots of battles with myself and my reactions, but the more I practiced the more I understood and was able to "dial down" and cooperate with the Spirit.

During the signs and wonders conference in Harrogate, England, last November I received a lot of blessing. However, there was a moment during a meeting when I received an anointing for ministry and since then have known a whole new freedom and more healings have begun to happen. This was very timely, as I was about to be made an elder in our church with responsibilities for training people in the use of spiritual gifts, especially in how to pray for the sick.

One of the things that happened was the healing of a physical complaint. Up until Harrogate, people I prayed for were getting healed emotionally but not physically. The physical healing happened like this. A woman came for prayer because someone in attendance had a word of knowledge about migraine. It was her first visit to the church. The time of worship had overwhelmed her and she was full of faith: it was written all over her face. We prayed for the migraine but could not tell if there was any improvement as she was not suffering from a headache that evening. When we had finished she said, "While you are at it, could you pray for my jaw?" How could we refuse when her faith was so evident? The left upper part of her jaw had been damaged in an accident and she was unable to move the lower jaw sideways; her bite was also affected. We laid hands on the damaged area and spoke healing to the bone in the name of Jesus. In about three minutes she was able to move her lower jaw back and forth and her bite returned to normal. The only difficulty was her tongue, which did not immediately adjust to the new situation, causing her to lisp as she spoke! Then she wanted us to pray for her nose—only because she didn't like the shape of it. We told her we weren't plastic surgeons! She left the church saying she was going to bring her husband as soon as possible. He arrived two weeks later and came forward for prayer after hearing a word of knowledge about his condition. They were both led to Christ. Power evangelism was beginning to happen.

In praying for the sick there seem to be stages that those who are learning to pray go through. The only way one enters the next stage is to be faithful in the one before. It's a case of not giving up, backing out, or looking for a way of escape. Instead, keep on praying, asking questions of others, listening to the Spirit, and studying the Scriptures. Jesus had to learn too, and obviously he learned well, but his disciples struggled and their recorded failures have been an encouragement to me; I see theirs and mine as part of a normal learning process.

The Third Wave has only just begun. Where it will end only God knows. Learning to ride that wave has been the most challenging experience of my life so far. I know I shall continue to take tumbles, feel overwhelmed, embarrassed, out of my depth, a total failure, and so forth, but God will always be waiting to help me back up again if I am willing to let him. So, come Holy Spirit, come.

3

Renewing the Renewal

Dave Nodar

Dave Nodar, a Catholic layman, is senior coordinator of the Lamb of God, an ecumenical community in Baltimore, Maryland. He and his wife, Cheryl, have four children.

As senior coordinator of the Lamb of God, a charismatic, interdenominational Christian community in Baltimore, I've had the privilege and joy of experiencing two significant moves of God on the earth during my lifetime. From my own experience I'd like to share some of my personal background and roots in the charismatic renewal and also share about the effect of this current action of God referred to by C. Peter Wagner as "the Third Wave."

In March of 1971, when I was twenty years old, I got down on my knees and prayed with a young man who had been raised as a Jehovah's Witness and only recently become a Christian. This young man, without explanation of what was occurring, placed his hands on my head and began praying in tongues. This was probably similar to what had occurred in his own life a few months before when a sixty-five-year-old Baptist charismatic prayed with him to receive Christ. At one point, this young man said that I should pray aloud to the Lord Jesus. He didn't give me any presentation on how to accept Christ or teach me "the sinner's prayer"; he just said, "Pray to the Lord." So I prayed honestly from the depths of my being—"Jesus, help me." As the words left my lips, the presence of God came on me and I experienced him filling me with his Holy Spirit from head to foot. In response to the Lord Jesus' presence, I said, "Jesus, I never want to leave you again."

A Fairy Tale

You see, for several years as a teenager I had been lured out of the church and into the world by rock and roll groups like the Beatles and the Rolling Stones. As my teen years went by and I yielded more fully to the world, the flesh, and the devil, I became increasingly aware of the lack of purpose and direction in my life. Through a series of divine appointments the Lord brought me to my senses and the realization that the type of life-style I was living was certainly not where true life and purpose were to be found.

Shortly after asking Jesus to be Lord of my life, I started a Bible study with college-aged people. The meeting rapidly grew both in numbers and in diversity of people attending. There were young and old, hippies and straights, Catholics and Protestants, blue-collar and executive types—all joining together on the common ground of Jesus Christ as Lord. The meeting quickly evolved into a charismatic prayer meeting with time for praise and worship, for use of the spiritual gifts, and also for teaching. God was pouring out his Spirit in an extraordinary way. He was transforming people's lives. People with drug habits, immoral life-styles, or involvement in the occult were being set free and empowered to live holy lives. We saw people healed of physical illnesses as they turned to the Lord. Those with marriages that were falling apart were restored. People who were only living nominal Christian lives were empowered and renewed in their life in Christ.

For me all this was like a fairy tale. It was almost too good to be true. I was encountering the Lord and seeing my life and the lives of many others change. My initial reaction to all this was to think that it was an experience that was, for some reason, only occurring with a few people in Baltimore, Maryland. However, in a short time I came to understand that we were involved with a major outpouring of God's Holy Spirit throughout the world in the late 1960s and early 1970s. This outpouring of God's Spirit has been referred to by many as the "charismatic renewal" and by others as "the Jesus movement." God was pouring out his Spirit across denominational lines, bringing Christians from various traditions together under his lordship to worship him and to love one another. The Lord was having an impact on young people who had no involvement whatsoever in denominational Christianity, laying hold of their lives and radically transforming them and giving them purpose in life.

Christian Community

Many of us who were involved in the prayer meetings in the early 1970s recognized the ideals of love, unity, togetherness, and commitment that we had aspired to and yet had not experienced before accepting Christ. We saw that, in our commitment to Christ, these ideals could be realized because the Lord Jesus called us not only to commitment to himself, but also to his body to "be the new humanity" (Eph. 2:14, 15). And so, over the years, the Lord directed us in his calling for us and we evolved from a Bible study into a charismatic prayer meeting and eventually into an interdenominational Christian community.

We believed that the Lord wanted to restore to us and to all of his people vital elements of normal Christian life that were the inheritance of God's people. These included such things as a process of incorporating new members into the life of the body of Christ that would include pastoral care and small fellowship groupings and instruction in aspects of Christian life (like becoming a Christian; personal relationships in Christ; being single, married, or raising children in the Lord). We were convinced that the Lord called us not only to be busy doing, that is, being evangelistically minded and concerned for mission, but also that he was concerned about our being, that is, that he was concerned that there be a testimony of body life. So, the Lord called us to a community way of life in obedience to his command to love one another as he loved us. By this we hope all people will know that we are his disciples through an unselfish love for one another.

In the early 1970s we also felt the Lord call us to be an interdenominational community. We live in an age of much division in the body of Christ; the Lord's body is broken. There are many relationships within various churches and between churches that are filled with animosity and division. And so in this context, both prophetically and circumstantially, we felt the Lord call us to become not a denominational church, but rather a community of Protestants, Catholics, and Orthodox and Messianic Jewish believers who are supportive of each other's respective traditions. It is through our commitment to one another that we hope to live out the message that we are proclaiming that unity without uniformity can be realized in the Lord Jesus. We do this not by ignoring our differences nor by compromising the truth, but by discovering our common ground in Jesus.

As the years went by, we furthered our commitment to unity and to restoration of normal Christian life by formalizing our relationships with various communities around the world. Together we are known as the Sword of the Spirit, an international, interdenominational movement committed to the proclamation of the gospel and the equipping of God's people for ministry.

Stalled Growth

During the latter portion of the 1970s our primary focus was on building up our life together. While I maintain that this is something the Lord called us to, I also note that we ended up extending this focus too long in the internal direction. It is also worth mentioning that during the period 1980–1982 our evangelistic outreaches and programs were not doing very well, whereas in the 1970s our committed membership growth was rather consistent. By 1980 we had stalled and were growing insignificantly. Evangelism was no longer easy for us to do. While I think some of the problem can be attributed to the prolonged internal focus, I think that it is also possible that the outpouring of God's Spirit, known as the charismatic renewal in the late 1960s and 1970s, was in decline or ebb tide. However, that was all about to change, because the Lord was going to come again in power to us as a people.

In 1983 the Lord was speaking prophetically to many of the communities of the Sword of the Spirit about coming to renew us and also about giving us spiritual power in a new and significant way. I know, for me personally, the Lord was preparing my heart. I recognize that, regarding personal testimonies of evangelism and healing, I was really lacking and that for significant examples of God's power I was reaching back several years into my past to find good, charismatic "war" stories. While I never stopped sharing the good news with people or exercising the spiritual gifts, the circumstances for these opportunities were extremely limited. I noted, also, that my personal faith that someone would be physically healed as I prayed with them was very low. Our corporate batting average for deliverance and for inner healing (i.e., the Lord's salvation, bringing repentance and restoration regarding past experiences) was pretty good, and yet in the physical healing area we were seeing fewer results as time went on.

A New Wave

During the summer and early fall of 1984 the Lord started to send us ambassadors or heralds of a new wave of his action. In July a friend of mine from Lancaster, Pennsylvania, Glenn Leaman, visited with my family and mentioned how he had attended a conference on signs and wonders in Anaheim, California. Glenn began to share with me how the speaker, John Wimber, had spoken about spiritual gifts as a means of upbuilding the body of Christ not only at Christian worship services, but in evangelism as a means of releasing God's kingdom and bringing people to Christ. It was clear to me the conference had a significant impact on Glenn and yet the idea of the spiritual gifts being utilized as power for evangelism didn't really compute. I must confess that my orientation was toward a programmatic means of evangelism at this point, evangelism that uses rational arguments rather than demonstrations of the power of the Spirit. Even though I knew the Scriptures that dealt with the Lord confirming their words in the Acts of the Apostles, it really didn't register with me.

Shortly after this encounter with Glenn, I sent two of my fellow coordinators to a conference on spiritual gifts that John Wimber was holding in New York. Frankly, I didn't go to the conference myself because I thought I wouldn't be able to learn anything new about the spiritual gifts. I preferred to attend a conference that was on some new topic. However, when the brothers returned from the conference, they were changed and revolutionized by their experience there. Once again, as Glenn had shared, they also spoke about how the spiritual gifts were not only for building up Christians at worship services, but also as a means of empowering those in Christ to minister the kingdom of God in evangelistic situations. They were not only impressed by the teaching that John Wimber delivered, but by the demonstration of power that occurred at the conference.

One particular example that moved the brothers deeply was a time of intercession for the brokenness of the body of Christ, which, as I mentioned, was very dear and important to us in our own calling as a community. The time of intercession wasn't just a time of praying petitions, but a time when God's power came in a profound way directly to the Christians who were at this conference. The brothers I sent felt driven to their knees and saw and experienced personally tremendous grieving for the brokenness and disunity that we presently experience among us as the body of Christ.

As a result of what had occurred with these two brothers of mine, I began listening to a series of tapes on healing by John Wimber. As I listened to the talks, I was drawn to the message that John spoke. His simple, encouraging approach that healing was to be normative and that it was for all Christians was something I really believed and wanted to see. And as he talked about the importance of obedience to God's word and the importance of persistence in praying for healing, I was struck with how we had been "knocked off our horse" in this area of Christian life by the reality of a few significant failures with brothers and sisters who were very sick. As a result of a failure to see any improvement in the health, we had become significantly discouraged. John's encouragement on the tapes in his call to have faith in God's faithfulness was stirring something deep within me.

Renewal

The fall of 1984 was a tremendous period of time for us as a community, because it was the beginning of a new move of God's Holy Spirit renewing and reviving us in the Lamb of God. And it was ushered in by repentance. As we gathered for times of prayer, the Lord was pointing out to us various sins in our hearts corporately and individually, areas of self-righteousness, areas of control, and areas of hypocrisy. As he was bringing these to light, the Lord began to show me personally the sins of my own heart. For example, while speaking in London on one occasion, I noticed the significant number of punk rockers in that city. Frankly, in my heart, I knew I didn't believe they could come to Christ. As I recognized that kind of attitude in my heart, I felt the Lord remind me of the type of person I had been when I first came to the Lord. I came to see in my heart that certain people who were really my brothers and sisters in Christ I considered problem people. In one particular worship gathering, as I looked at one individual whom I knew I considered a problem person, I experienced the presence of God come on this person. My reaction in my heart, regretfully, was, "Lord, this can't be. You don't understand." And then the Lord responded to me, "No, Dave, *you* don't understand. This person isn't a problem person. He's a brother who has a problem and I love him very much." In these kinds of situations God was breaking up the fallow ground. He was breaking up my hardness of heart and showing me that I had not only forgotten where I had personally come from, but also why I was here.

God was dealing with my heart. He was stirring me in the depths of my being. I was beginning to experience a renewed sensitivity to the Holy Spirit. Paul reminded Timothy in 2 Timothy 1:6. "Fan into flame the gift of God which is in you through the laying on of my hands." I could sense the Lord stirring and compelling me out of love not only to pastorally care for my brothers and sisters in Christ, but also to extend his love to those around me who didn't know him. Christ is the power of God and the wisdom of God (1 Cor. 1:24). I recognized that the Lord had blessed us with wisdom for living the Christian life in the Lamb of God and the Sword of the Spirit. But the Lord also wanted us to recognize that he is the power of God and that he wants to regularly intervene supernaturally in the lives of his people and through his people to advance his reign.

During the fall of 1984 and early winter 1985 I saw this beautifully illustrated as I had the opportunity to speak at pastoral renewal conferences in the United States. Another speaker was Kevin Springer. A personal friend of mine, Kevin had also been dramatically affected by the Lord's action through the ministry of John Wimber. These conferences are geared at sharing sound Christian pastoral wisdom with other Christian leaders. At the end of each of these conferences we took the opportunity to pray for the leaders who attended to be strengthened, encouraged, and empowered by the Holy Spirit. As we moved into these prayer sessions, I could see that Kevin was renewed in his own sensitivity to the Holy Spirit. He was able to yield to the Lord giving him insights for particular needs, concerns, and sins in the lives of the various leaders who were there in a way that helped them appropriate more of the Lord's life. Just being in those situations of prayer did a lot to renew me personally as well as activate the use of the spiritual gifts through me.

Gifts for Everyone

During that period of time Kevin mentioned to me that there was a conference to be held in Anaheim in February of 1985 and that, if possible, I should try to attend. I had such a longing in my heart, such a desire to serve the Lord's people with more of God's power, that as soon as he said that, I knew that I should attend. So I told the other coordinators in our community that I wanted to attend this conference. They not only agreed but felt that they all should attend as well. We also invited any other members of the community to attend who could. As a result, eleven other members chose to go to the conference as well.

The conference, which was on signs and wonders, was a turning point for us in our renewal and advance in the new movement of the Holy Spirit. One area of significant change for us was a shift from pastoral to lay ministry. Normally most ministry occurred through pastoral leaders in our community; we saw, however, the opportunity for brothers and sisters to serve one another through the spiritual gifts in a way that would bear more fruit and give much more sense of purpose to the individual members of our community.

For example, one of the women, named Evelyn, who went to the conference with us was a widow. Her husband had died a couple of years before and she was able to lay hold of a renewed sense of purpose and identity in the Lord as a result of being at the conference. When she returned to Baltimore from the conference, she prayed with one of her sons for a physical problem and he was healed. The word got out to some other friends about this. Another family had a daughter who had been born with one entire side of her body smaller than the other. The mother of this girl called Evelyn and asked her if she would come pray with her; Evelyn went and prayed and the power of God came upon this girl. As she prayed down the side of the girl's body, the Lord worked a miracle and the bones grew out as she prayed, so that both sides of her body matched up evenly in size. God used Evelyn in a miraculous way but, even more importantly, it renewed in her a sense of purpose and mission as a daughter of God.

I was personally struck by the number of young people at the conference. People with long hair, guys with earrings, girls in clothing that I didn't think was acceptable for Christians were right in the midst of the worship and were praising God and praying for one another. It struck my heart that, while I maintained a firm conviction in the importance of Christians having a sound character and being mature in Christ, it wasn't as if they had to be perfect before they could do anything! These young people who looked as if they had just recently come to Christ were being trained in using the spiritual gifts and praying for one another in a way that would help to move them ahead in holiness as well.

During the conference I had the opportunity to have lunch with John Wimber, at which time John prayed with me specifically for the areas that I longed for in my heart, although I hadn't mentioned them to him. He prayed that I would be empowered by the Lord to minister his life in a more significant way to those around me. And while at the time I didn't *experience* anything noticeable, I knew something had changed and that something became apparent once I was actually in the situation where I could minister the Lord's life—I received the gift of discernment of spirits. It was operating in a way that I was able to see the Holy Spirit coming upon people for ministry or see evil spirits working on people—something that I never experienced prior to contact with John's ministry. Seeing John operate in this gift and then praying with me actually released the faith and released the spiritual gift to operate in me as well.

Over the next year and a half I had a number of opportunities to be with John and Carol Wimber. John told me that his desire was to see other people lay hold of all that God was doing in this new movement of his Holy Spirit and be equipped so that they, in turn, could give it away to others. Being with John in a number of ministry situations gave me insight and helped me understand some of the dynamics of how he and those with him ministered in the Holy Spirit. Something has been imparted to me that has changed my life and my ministry. I am indebted to John, whom God has used to herald a new wave of the Holy Spirit. Over the last couple of years as I've traveled and had opportunities to speak at various conferences in the United States and other countries, I've seen the Lord emphasizing certain areas of Christian life that are biblical and, therefore, timeless. However, I believe the Lord is focusing on certain areas as new works of the Holy Spirit. I'd like to share with you three in particular.

Fatherhood

The first has to do with a fresh revelation or for many a new revelation of the fatherhood of God and how much he deeply loves his children. There really is a renewed sense of calling to prayer in the body of Christ today. In many places where I speak I see the Holy Spirit drawing people to himself and the Lord revealing to his people more about himself. I've been struck with how many people, as they're renewed and experience God bringing his rule upon their lives, come to encounter the Lord in a more intimate and personal way. In one situation where we spent some time praying and the Holy Spirit came in power, one man began sobbing uncontrollably, something I knew to be atypical for his personality. When I asked him what the Lord was doing with him, he tried to regain control of himself and all he could get out amidst sobs was, "He [God] called me son." In many situations like this one, I've seen people not only have such a personal experience, but this experience also effects a significant change in their lives.

I've noticed that many Christians don't have a proper sense of their position or standing before God, the Father, that is, that he accepts them in Jesus Christ. It's not something they can merit or work up to, but it's something that has been accomplished through what Christ Jesus has done. The Lord, both through the truth of his word and the revelation of his Holy Spirit, wants people to have an adequate foundation in the knowledge of his love for them as the basis of their living in Christ and serving through him. Currently, in many situations, I'm seeing God bring this important truth to light in the lives of his people.

Proclamation

The second area in which I feel the Lord speaking to his people is the clear proclamation of the good news of the kingdom of God, that is, that the Lord Jesus wants his people to continue his ministry, demonstrating both through word as well as through deed that the kingdom of God, the rule of God, is now at hand. It's breaking into this present evil age in which we live. For many Christians nowadays the kingdom of God is something to look forward to. While that's true, we're also supposed to be ambassadors proclaiming that the good news of God is at hand. Just as the Lord empowered the disciples to be witnesses, we too are to be witnesses in holiness of life, in life together as the new humanity.

We are also supposed to demonstrate, personally and corporately, the reality of the rule of God breaking in and destroying the works of the devil. One of the significant aspects of the proclamation of the Good News is that it's for anytime and anywhere.

In 1980 we started to see the Lord come in power in our community gatherings, bringing healing. At a discussion with our coordinators, we tried to work out how to keep it going and yet at the same time do all the other things that we needed to do. My conclusion was that we should try to have a healing meeting once every three months or so. While that may have been an adequate suggestion, it was based on misunderstanding of the fact that the Lord wants to bring his rule, his power to bear on people anytime and anywhere. The Lord isn't inhibited from manifesting his rule in situations other than Christian services. While Jesus ministered in power in the synagogues during his life on earth, he also ministered in the marketplace frequently. And so I've been changed, and we as a community have been changed, to be sensitive and open to the Holy Spirit using us anytime and anywhere, whether it's in school, on the job, in our neighborhoods, in the grocery stores, wherever. He's made us sensitive to the fact that we belong to him; we're his servants; we're ambassadors of his kingdom. He wants to use us if only we'll be obedient to him and sensitive to the Holy Spirit.

Recently, several members of our community had the opportunity to speak on a college campus. There the Lord revealed the hearts of students, showing us through the exercise of the word of knowledge areas of sin, addictions, feelings of rejection, and so forth. These students encountered the finger of God disclosing the secrets of their hearts, bypassing their arguments and demonstrating his rule at hand, and bringing his love and forgiveness to them.

I believe that the Lord wants to bring his kingdom and his rule to bear much more significantly in the lives of Christians, so that in turn they might bring his rule to bear upon those around them. In our community life, we've seen a number of changes already; I believe there will be many more to come as we allow the power of God to affect our personal lives in the life of the community. For example, for several years now one of our major concerns has been to see our teenagers and our young adults living in the Lord, although we haven't been overly successful. Over the last two years, a group of fathers have gathered weekly to intercede on behalf of the young people of our community. Then, in the summer of 1986, without any reason for this coming to mind, I felt the Lord say to me, "I'm going to begin to work in power among the young of the community." At the time there was no reason to believe that was the case, but I knew with certainty that the Lord had spoken to me and that it was going to occur. Sure enough, over the last six months, we've seen a dramatic change and over two-thirds of our young adults have turned to Christ in a significant way; they are banding together with the desire to have fellowship and to get the support to live strong, Christian lives. While there were supports in the past for our young adults to live Christian lives, I'd have to say that both intercessory prayer and new openness in understanding the kingdom of God turned this situation around for us. The Lord Jesus wants to rule his people. He also wants us to be his servant people through whom he is advancing his kingdom in our day and demonstrating the good news in word and works, which leads me to the third area of emphasis.

All God's People

I believe the Lord wants to release his whole body to serve—not just leaders, not just people with special giftings, but all of his people are to serve him in the power of his Holy Spirit. This is all very exciting to me. I'm seeing brothers and sisters renewed in their dedication to Jesus as Lord of their lives and renewed in zeal to do the works that he's already prepared in advance for them.

As a leader, I want to be able to train his people in the Christian life, to help to bring them to maturity, and at the same time be able to release them, not hold them back from being able to serve the Lord in the power of his Holy Spirit. As the Lord deepens our knowledge of him personally, as he teaches us about the rule of God and gives us the ability to proclaim it both in word and by demonstration of power, and as the pastoral leadership of our community helps to release brothers and sisters to serve the Lord, we're seeing increased vitality in our life together. Moreover, we're seeing new people added to our number regularly.

Since we began experiencing renewal in our life in the fall of 1984, there's been a consistent surge of growth in our life. As a people, we're faced with two possibilities. We can attempt to be happy and comfortable and live life together as God has already given it to us, or we can be a militant, active, aggressive servant people of God through whom he's advancing his kingdom here in Baltimore. We don't want to settle for less, because we know just being ourselves and living our life isn't what God has called us to be and to do. He's purified us so that we might be a people of his own who are eager to do good deeds (Titus 2:14). We want to see our Father's will coming in the earth today. We want to see heaven coming to earth. We know that God has equipped us with his power and with his wisdom in order to serve him effectively.

This yielding ourselves more to the rule of God in our lives personally and as churches, communities, and fellowships is a process that occurs over years. As the senior coordinator of our community, I recognize that if I wasn't personally committed to yielding to the Holy Spirit in the ways that I've been talking about and wasn't personally encouraging and modeling those ways, it wouldn't happen. And so, any Christian leaders reading this must recognize that we can't just come up with some good notes or some tapes and then regurgitate the material. The kingdom of God has to come to bear in *our* lives, where we resolve that we're going to be obedient servants of God and do his will daily.

Over the last couple of years, I've spoken to groups of pastors and to large conferences with thousands in attendance. I have had the privilege of praying for the Holy Spirit to come and have with joy and awe seen him come bringing healing, deliverance, and renewal to people. With power the Lord comes to demonstrate his love and compassion for humanity and for the reality that the rule of God is at hand. I'm so thankful for what the Lord has done in me. I encourage you to seize the opportunity of this season of grace we're in. Draw close to the Lord. Put your faith in his unfailing love. Give yourself to him as servants of his will. The Lord wants to renew and rule his people. He wants to thrust us out into the world equipped with his wisdom and power to advance his kingdom. Let's let him do it!

II

Worldview Encounters

Between them the three men contributing to this section have written over fifty books and hold four doctoral degrees. They are bright fellows, well trained in theology and Western rationalism. It is perhaps because of their educational backgrounds that they began to look more closely at their presuppositions—their worldviews—when they were challenged by Christians from other cultures, either in the classroom or on the mission field. I could easily have placed all of their stories in the missionary section of this book, but their awareness of the influence of worldviews provided a unique opportunity to look at this key area separately.

4

God Wasn't Pulling My Leg

C. Peter Wagner

C. Peter Wagner is the Donald A. McGavran professor of church growth at the Fuller Theological Seminary in Pasadena, California, where he has taught since 1971. Before that he served as a missionary to Bolivia for sixteen years. He holds a Ph.D. in Social Ethics from the University of Southern California and has published twenty-seven works. He and his wife, Doris, have two children and two grandchildren.

I have now joined the ranks of those who believe that supernatural power, miracles, and signs and wonders are important components in a strategy to evangelize today's world. I like John Wimber's term "power evangelism," but it wasn't always like that. Let me explain.

I have been an ordained minister for over thirty years. Since the day I was born again, at age 19 in 1950, I have attempted to serve Jesus Christ as my Lord. Unlike many of my friends, I myself cannot remember a day in which I doubted that God exists, or that Jesus died on the cross for my sins, or that the Bible is true, or that I was called into full-time Christian service. I have not been a supersaint, but my Christian life has been fairly consistent and probably at least average. How could it be, then, that only in the past few years have I begun to discover that the God I have been serving throughout my life is truly a God of power?

The Great Commission

The central focus of my Christian life has been the Great Commission, God's command to make disciples of all nations. When my wife,

Doris, led me to Christ some months before we were married, she had already committed her life to missionary work. I joined her, and the same night I was saved I promised God I would be a missionary. We traveled across country from our home in upstate New York to southern California, where I enrolled in Fuller Seminary and she attended Biola College in preparation for the mission field. After graduation and my ordination, we launched out for sixteen years of missionary work in Bolivia.

Our first term was spent in the jungles of eastern Bolivia, toward the Brazilian border. I ran a small Bible institute, evangelized, planted a church, spoke at Bible conferences, and encouraged Bolivian pastors. Our second and third terms took us out of the tropics and into the temperate Andes Mountains in the city of Cochabamba. There I spent most of my time teaching in seminary and in mission administration, directing the mission.

In 1967 I came in contact with an extraordinary man, Donald McGavran, who was the founder of the Fuller School of World Mission. I took a degree under him at Fuller and was introduced to the church growth movement, which totally changed my way of thinking about missions and world evangelization. As I look back now, I see that besides my wife, who led me to Christ, the two individuals whom God has most used to influence my Christian life are McGavran and John Wimber, who came into the picture ten years later. The upshot of spending a year with Donald McGavran was that he invited me to become his understudy in church growth on the Fuller faculty, so eventually our family moved from Bolivia to Pasadena, California, where we have been since 1971.

My life text was and is Matthew 28:19-20: "Go therefore and make disciples of all the nations, baptizing them in the name of the Father and of the Son and of the Holy Spirit, teaching them to observe all things I have commanded you." I am so committed to this text that when I had the opportunity to order personalized California license plates for my car, I ordered MT 28:19. Then awhile later when Doris, who has served as my personal secretary since 1964, got a car, she joined me and ordered MT 28:20. So wherever we go, we go with the Great Commission.

Where Was the Power?

The strange thing was that in all those sixteen years as a missionary, I never saw a very important connection between Matthew 28:18 and Matthew 28:19-20. Jesus' statement of the Great Commission begins with the words, "All authority has been given to Me in heaven and earth." Then the rest goes on with "therefore." I didn't really know what the "therefore" was there for.

That word "authority" is *exousia* in the Greek. It is frequently translated "power" as well as "authority." It is an important word because it connotes derived power, not inherent power as in another New Testament word, *dunamis*. Not only was Jesus given this *exousia* power by the Father, as he said in Matthew 28:18, but he also passed it on to his disciples. For example, the first time he sent the Twelve out on their own, Jesus "gave them power [*exousia*] over unclean spirits, to cast them out, and to heal all kinds of sickness and all kinds of disease" (Matt. 10:1). The "therefore" indicates that there is some link between this and the execution of the Great Commission.

Part of the Great Commission is "teaching them to observe all things that I have commanded you." Obviously some things Jesus commanded his disciples from time to time have no direct application in most cases today. Going to the Jews rather than to Gentiles or Samaritans (Matt. 10:5-6) is one case in point. Not taking any money or extra clothing (Matt. 10:9-10) is another. But preaching that "the kingdom of heaven is at hand" (Matt. 10:7) is something else, something that we today are expected to do. And, as I see it now, so is "Heal the sick, raise the dead, cleanse those who have leprosy, drive out demons" (Matt. 10:8). Using the *exousia* power that Jesus gives us should be part and parcel of fulfilling the Great Commission. But during sixteen years on the mission field I cannot remember even once when that power was channeled through me for healing the sick or casting out demons.

Four Roadblocks to Power

For some time now I have been attempting to answer the question: Why? In all honesty I do not think it was due to a lack of faith or a low level of dedication to Jesus as Lord. But there were at least four roadblocks keeping me from discovering the power:

1. I was a dispensationalist. The Bibles I used, both in English and Spanish, had an editor's footnote in 1 Corinthians 13 that said the "sign" gifts such as tongues and healings and miracles went out of use right after the apostolic age. I knew the difference between a footnote and the text, but I had been thoroughly taught that since we now had the canon of Scripture, we no longer needed signs and wonders to draw the attention of unbelievers to Jesus. I believed that the kingdom of God was something for the future, not for the present.

2. I was anti-Pentecostal. In my circles it was fashionable to regard Pentecostals as frauds. We admitted that they probably would end up in heaven, but we considered that judgment an act of Christian generosity since their theology seemed so shallow. I had an aversion, rather than any appreciation, for their style of ministry. When a Pentecostal healer would come to Cochabamba, I would warn the people in my church not to go. Much to my dismay, they went anyhow. And worse yet, some were healed. I remained unimpressed.

3. I had a limited view of power. I believed in the power of God, but I had been taught that it was power for salvation and for living a holy life. Talking about any power beyond that was theologically suspect. It was something those poor Pentecostals did.

4. My worldview was shaped by secular humanism. From my new perspective I am increasingly amazed at the degree to which secular humanism, which is so deeply entrenched in our contemporary American culture, has penetrated our Christian schools and churches and seminaries and literature. As my colleague Paul G. Hiebert has pointed out on many occasions, we missionaries have often unsuspectingly served as agents of secularization as we have gone to minister to Third World cultures. I certainly was doing that. I can

remember feeling that part of my missionary work was to convince people that diseases were caused by germs, not, as they superstitiously thought, by evil spirits. They must have wondered how I could promote God on one hand and remove the supernatural from daily life on the other.

Now things have changed. Now I experience God's power operating through healing the sick and casting out demons as a regular part of my ministry. I am no longer a dispensationalist or anti-Pentecostal. What happened to change the situation? I went through what we now call "a paradigm shift." It was a very gradual process that included four stages.

E. Stanley Jones

The first stage was my encounter with E. Stanley Jones, the famous Methodist missionary to India. Back in the mid-sixties, E. Stanley Jones had been invited to Bolivia by the local Methodists. Not only was I a dispensationalist then, but I was a separatist fundamentalist. I had been taught in seminary that E. Stanley Jones was a liberal, and I wanted no association with him. Our mission, along with several others, voted in the citywide ministerial association not to welcome Jones to Cochabamba. The Methodists were left on their own.

But much to my surprise, one of our senior missionaries, a former director of the mission and a saint of God, quietly slipped out to Jones's first meeting. He told me the next day that Jones was no liberal, but that he preached a biblical gospel message and gave an evangelistic invitation for people to be saved. My friend was as fundamentalist as I, so I trusted his judgment. He aroused my curiosity to say the least, so the next night Doris and I went.

Since I was one who publicly voted against Jones, I took pains to go to his meeting under cover of darkness, to arrive late, and to sit in the back of the room. The meeting turned out to be an old-fashioned healing service with an invitation at the end for people who needed healing to come forward for prayer.

I badly needed healing. I had developed a cyst on my neck that had required surgery to remove. I am not an ideal medical patient, and I almost died when I went into shock shortly after the operation. The surgeon said it had been an extremely close call. But to make matters worse, the incision would not heal. For weeks it had been a runny, pus-filled sore. And just a couple of days previously the doctor had told me he was going to have to schedule another surgery. That was the last thing I wanted.

So there I was, listening to E. Stanley Jones's invitation for divine healing. His preaching had allowed me to bypass some of my anti-Pentecostal fears and had built my faith. But I was the mission director and I wasn't supposed to be in the meeting, so I didn't move. When several had gone forward for ministry, Jones did a wonderful thing. He said, "I know there are others who need healing but for one reason or another you have not felt free to come forward. Just relax, because I am going to pray for you also." I took that personally, and as he prayed I had the faith to trust God to heal that incision.

When we got home I took the bandage off. The sore was still open and runny, but I went to bed without the bandage. The next morning it was completely well and has been so until today. My paradigm began to shift—but only slightly.

Pentecostals are Okay

The second stage involved church growth research. Part of what Donald McGavran had taught me in the late sixties was to study growing churches to discover church growth principles that in turn could be applied to other churches. I had worked in Latin America enough by then to realize that those Pentecostal churches I didn't like very much were by far the fastest growing in the region. In fact, whereas perhaps 20 percent of Latin American evangelicals were Pentecostals in 1950, currently the figure is over 75 percent. This was a phenomenon a church growth leader could not ignore, but I knew that with my reputation I could not show any interest in the Pentecostal churches in Bolivia. Bruno Frigoli, an Assemblies of God missionary, was one of my worst enemies. However, right over on the other side of the Andes Mountains in Chile was a large group of Pentecostals showing explosive growth—no one knew me there.

So with a certain amount of trepidation, I flew over the mountains to Chile and attended a few Pentecostal services. To my amazement these people behaved like true born-again Christians. I observed the fruit of the Spirit. I talked to their leaders and discovered men and women of God. I asked theological questions and got sensible answers. The one big difference was their worship services. Unlike most of the believers in our churches in Bolivia, they were actually having fun in church! They were singing and dancing in the Spirit, clapping their hands, and holding their arms up in the air. Before I knew it, I decided to give it a try, and it really was enjoyable. I heard some tongues and prophecies and began to think that perhaps those gifts did not go out with the apostles after all.

The first thing I did was to go back home and make friends with Bruno Frigoli. And soon afterward we moved back to the United States to begin teaching at Fuller. I kept researching Latin American Pentecostals and wrote a book on them now called *Spiritual Power and Church Growth*. Writing the book helped me take another large step toward a paradigm shift. And, I am now happy to say, reading it has helped hundreds of others to do the same thing.

Work Among Pentecostals

The third stage in shifting my paradigm came about through a period of ministry in the mid-seventies with the Church of God in Cleveland, Tennessee. Their leaders invited me to help them understand church growth principles, which I attempted to do. But this was the first classical Pentecostal denomination I had made contact with over an extended period of time. While they were paying me to teach them, little did they know that I was learning as much as I was teaching. The men and women of God whom I met there showed me that they were in touch with a dimension of the power of God that I needed. Every time I visited them I came home spiritually refreshed. At times I found myself wishing I were a Pentecostal!

John Wimber Appears

The fourth and final stage of my paradigm shift came as a result of my contact with John Wimber. When I first met John Wimber in 1975 he was a Quaker pastor who had enrolled in my Doctor of Ministry church growth course. He had already gained a reputation for catalyzing positive growth dynamics in Yorba Linda Friends Church, so I recognized his name when I called the roll. We got to know each other, and after the first week he said, "I've really always known these things you've been teaching, but I never knew what to call them." By the end of the second week I knew that John had an unusually high aptitude as a church growth practitioner and consultant; he was a person I needed.

During the decade of the seventies, I directed the Fuller Evangelistic Association and by the middle of the decade I had begun the process of establishing what is now known as the Charles E. Fuller Institute of Evangelism and Church Growth. I was doing well as a church growth theoretician, but I needed to team up with a practitioner who could figure out how to apply church growth principles to the grass roots where they would do the most good. John was the person, and I persuaded him to leave his pastorate and come to work for me. John got the Fuller Institute off to a fine start, and we became fast personal friends with a great admiration for each other's gifts and ministries. With regard to spiritual power we were both about the same—traditional straight-line evangelicals. We admired Pentecostals and charismatics, but from a distance. I had a small advantage over John in those days, since I did use a prayer language from time to time and had done so for some years. John had spoken in tongues once as a new Christian, but was told he shouldn't do it again. We never discussed it in those days, nor did I regard it as a central factor in my spiritual life.

Then came John's call to plant a new church. I supported the idea at first, thinking it would be a little sideline that would keep him out of trouble on the weekends when he wasn't counseling with pastors. Little did I know that it would eventually grow into Vineyard Christian Fellowship of Anaheim with over five thousand members. When God began to bless the church with extraordinary growth, John was forced to resign his position with the Fuller Institute in 1977. God knew about that too and had prepared Carl George to take John's place and the institute has moved along well since. John and I remained close friends and John continued to help me teach my Doctor of Ministry course called Church Growth II every August.

I became vaguely aware that John had begun to pray for the sick and see God heal people through 1978 and 1979 and 1980. Curious, I visited the church on a Sunday night now and then when it was in the gymnasium of Canyon High School. In 1981 John suggested that perhaps we could use one of our mornings in Church Growth II for a lecture on "Signs, Wonders and Church Growth." If the suggestion had come from any number of other people, I might have hesitated. But I knew John well and he had such high integrity and credibility that I gave him the green light. Since it was to be the first such class on the subject in the history of the seminary, I invited the dean of our School of World Mission, Paul E. Pierson, to sit in.

From a Spectator to a Participant

Although it was nothing along the lines that Pierson and I had ever heard before, we were both impressed. As we were debriefing over lunch, John mentioned that he had collected much more material on the subject and we began discussing the possibilities of teaching a whole course on signs and wonders in our regular School of World Mission curriculum. Over the next few months the School of World Mission faculty discussed the matter at length and finally decided to introduce a course called "MC510 Signs, Wonders and Church Growth." I was to be the professor of record, and John was to do most of the teaching.

I went to the class, which began in January 1982, but as a spectator.

I sat in the last row to watch John "doin' the stuff." I had no intention of becoming a participant in the kind of ministry John was talking about.

But this all changed about the third week. When the teaching was over and the ministry time was beginning, John said, "Is there anyone here who needs prayer for physical healing?" Before I knew it, my hand was in the air. For several years I had been under treatment for high blood pressure and I was taking three pills a day. John had me sit on a stool and began to pray with the class looking on. I felt a tremendous sense of peace come over me. I became so relaxed that I thought I might fall off the stool. I dimly heard John saying to the class, "The Holy Spirit is on him. Can you see the Holy Spirit on him?" How long I was there I don't know, but it must have been the better part of ten minutes. John told me he felt God ministering to me, but I was not to go off the medication until I had permission from the doctor.

In a few days I went to my doctor and he was surprised to see my blood pressure so low. I asked him if he wanted to hear what happened, and he did. When I had told him the story, he said, "That's very interesting. I know that much can happen under hypnosis!" He took me off the medication gradually, and in a few months I was taking none.

This is what it took to finish my process of moving from a skeptic to a spectator to a participant. I started laying hands on the sick and learning how to minister to them in the name of Jesus. Not many got well at first, but enough did to encourage me. Soon praying for the sick was a permanent part of my Christian life, even though at that time I did not yet have the gift of healing.

The 120 Fellowship

God, I believe, wanted my ministry to the sick to increase in a more formal or structured way. In the summer of 1982, after the first session of "Signs, Wonders and Church Growth" had ended, I helped start a new adult Sunday school class in my church, Lake

Avenue Congregational Church in Pasadena, California. Our conscious planning did not anticipate that the class would become a center for ministry to the sick, but it did so happen that the week before the new class was to begin I was asked to fill the church pulpit for all three morning services while Pastor Paul Cedar was on vacation. I chose to share with the whole congregation what God was doing to bring in the harvest around the world and part of this, quite naturally, was telling stories about supernatural signs and wonders.

Now, Lake Avenue Congregational Church is a very traditional evangelical church. It is ninety years old and has grown during every one of its nine decades to a church of over four thousand members with over three thousand in attendance. Evangelical celebrities such as Wilbur M. Smith, Charles Woodbridge, David Allan Hubbard, Harold Lindsell, Ted Engstrom, Ralph Winter, Ed Dayton, and many others have taught adult Sunday school there. While it has not been an anticharismatic church, it would be characterized as noncharismatic.

My sermon sharing some of the signs and wonders going on in the world sparked the interest of many church members, and the first class had an attendance of 88. Through the years the class, now called The 120 Fellowship, has been up and down and is stabilized at around 100 on the rolls with an attendance of 80 to 100. Without my even asking for it, God brought some unusually gifted people to the class. I began to notice gifts of intercession, pastoring, healing, exorcism, prophecy, administration, discernment of spirits, words of knowledge, and many others. Several class members began to make it a habit of attending Anaheim Vineyard on Sunday nights. I said, "We go to Vineyard on Sunday nights to get charged up and come to Lake on Sunday mornings to discharge!"

The "Third Wave"

Among the gifted people were George Eckart and Cathy Schaller, whom I put in charge of the class prayer team. Both are disciples of John Wimber. They began a regular time of ministry to the sick after class on Sunday mornings that has continued through the years. God has allowed us to exercise a significant healing ministry in a traditional evangelical church largely because the pastor, Paul A. Cedar, is not only supportive of The 120 Fellowship but also combines the wisdom to know what it should do and what it should not do; and by design we avoid allowing the class to be characterized as "charismatic." Because we feel that the label "charismatic" does not fit us, we needed some alternative description, so we coined the phrase "Third Wave." By it we mean that we are experiencing supernatural power similar to that in the Pentecostal movement (First Wave) and charismatic movement (Second Wave) without being or intending to become part of either of them.

Whether the name "Third Wave" will stick or not remains to be seen. However, a strong confirmation of the ministry itself came in November 1983 when I received five separate prophecies from five independent sources, all bringing a similar message. God apparently was appointing me to be one of his messengers to spread the knowledge of his power to those who do not yet experience it for the building of the church of Jesus Christ. And I am to do it in a non-Pentecostal, noncharismatic way.

But the prophecies also warned that the enemy would attack, and he has. Spiritual warfare is now an ongoing experience, predictably so since the Lord has also told me that I am high on Satan's hit list. In January 1983 the power of an evil spirit that had been causing debilitating headaches for years was broken after counsel from John Wimber. In March the devil tried to kill me by pulling a ladder out from under me and causing me to take a ten-foot free fall, neck first, onto a concrete floor. I am convinced I would be dead now had it not been for intercessory prayer by Cathy Schaller, who was ten miles away, at exactly that moment. This caused us to suspect that spirits might have been assigned to our house, and it was later confirmed when my wife, Doris, actually saw one in our bedroom. Led by the Holy Spirit, George Eckart and Cathy Schaller used their gifts of discernment and exorcism to rid the house of a number of afflicting spirits and they have not bothered us since.

The Gift of Healing

I received my gift of healing in August 1984 through the ministry of Pastor Fred Luthy of Big Rapids, Michigan. I met Fred, a Lutheran pastor, in a Doctor of Ministry course I was teaching in Cleveland, Ohio, in 1983. With my encouragement, Fred, who has a powerful gift of healing, was running an informal healing seminar during the breaks in my church growth class. We saw many miraculous works of God during those two weeks and Fred became a close friend.

Luthy came to Pasadena for his Church Growth II course in August 1984. There he and John Wimber met and compared notes for the first time. I also invited Fred to come to my home to meet with the leadership of my 120 Fellowship prayer team. Toward the end of the meeting he suggested that we pray for the sick and soon discovered that one of the people had a short leg. I was watching to see what would happen, when Luthy said, "I think God wants you to pray for this leg." So I did and it instantly lengthened. Two other similar cases were healed that day.

I don't believe in the quick conclusion that being used for healing a few times indicates that you have the gift of healing. So I said to myself and others that I would experiment with it for the rest of the year, praying that God would show me clearly whether or not he had given me the gift over the next four months.

Many things happened over those four months, but two stand out in my mind. The first took place in a Vineyard conference that fall called "Wimber on Wagner." For the first time I received a word from the Lord to conduct a mass healing in the pastors' banquet. I obeyed, and fifty people who had leg, back, and other skeletal problems were instantly healed.

That fall, Paul Yonggi Cho, pastor of the world's largest church in Seoul, Korea, and a long-time friend of mine, came to Pasadena to deliver the annual Church Growth Lectures at Fuller Seminary. While I was with him he mentioned that he heard that God had given me a gift of lengthening legs and that he would like to see me do it. Sure enough, the next day God sent in an Egyptian Coptic pastor who had been run over by a train as a teenager and whose leg had been stiff, deformed, and short ever since. God moved powerfully, his leg lengthened, and he was able to stand on it for the first time since the accident.

Cho later told the story to his congregation in Seoul and it was heard by a deaconness whose hip sockets had been disintegrating. During the sermon she believed she heard God tell her to go to Pasadena to have Peter Wagner pray for her. She checked with Pastor Cho and he agreed, so she came. I didn't know she was on her way until after she had left Korea. She came into my office on a crutch, but she left walking. A week later, just before returning to Korea, she showed me X-rays taken before and after and pointed to places where new bone was growing.

By the end of the year, then, God had showed me that he had given me a gift of healing. Now I try to use it as much as possible for God's glory.

What Is It For?

Discovering the power is thrilling, but I need to keep reminding myself that supernatural power is not an end in itself. It is a means God has given us toward an end—toward the purpose of world evangelization. What John Wimber calls "power evangelism" is summarized in the end of the Gospel of John. The apostle mentions Jesus' signs and says that he has included a few of them in his gospel "that you may believe that Jesus is the Christ, the Son of God, and that believing you may have life in His name" (John 20:31).

I remain committed to the Great Commission. But better than ever before I now understand what Jesus meant when he said, "But you shall receive power when the Holy Spirit has come upon you; and you shall be witnesses to Me . . ." (Acts 1:8).

5

Shifting Worldviews, Sifting Attitudes

Charles Kraft

Charles Kraft is a professor at the School of World Mission, Fuller Seminary, Pasadena, California. He holds a Ph.D. in Anthropological Linguistics from Hartford Seminary and has served as a missionary to northern Nigeria. He has written thirteen books. Dr. Kraft and his wife, Marguerite, have four children. They attend an Evangelical Covenant Church.

It was late in 1981. As a senior member of the faculty of the School of World Mission, Fuller Seminary, I had voted to invite John Wimber to offer a course entitled "Signs, Wonders and Church Growth." My wife, Meg, and I decided to attend. We couldn't have foreseen it then, but we were on the verge of the most transforming experience we have ever known.

We had been brought up as "typical" evangelicals, I in an independent church with dispensational leanings in Connecticut and Meg as a "preacher's kid" in Indiana. We met at Wheaton College in 1949, got married in 1953, and had two children by 1955. By 1957 we had completed seminary and a year of specialized mission studies and were off to Nigeria to serve as pioneer church and language/Bible translation missionaries under the Brethren Church (Ashland, Ohio). We went out well trained in biblical studies, anthropology, and linguistics.

We were well prepared except, as it turned out, in the area the Nigerians considered the most important—their relationships with the spirit world. These spirits, they told me, cause disease, accidents, and death, hinder fertility of people, animals, and fields, bring drought, destroy relationships, harass the innocent, and the like.

The church leaders decided to focus in preaching on God's conquest of the spirits through Christ. But I could not help, for I was just plain ignorant in this area. Though I was open enough both to accept the reality of the spirit world and to appreciate its importance to the Nigerians, neither my anthropological nor my biblical and theological training had provided me with any constructive approaches to their felt need. The leaders did sometimes preach about the power of God to heal and deliver from demons. But there wasn't the kind of immediate response to their (or our) prayers that would lead outsiders to understand Christianity as superior to their old ways in the area of spiritual power.

There were other benefits to being Christian, however, and by the grace of God, many were coming into the kingdom. But most of these people "knew" there wasn't any power in Christianity to deal with such things as tragedies, infertility, relational breakdowns, troublesome weather, and the like. So they accommodated to the perceived weakness of Christianity and the ignorance of the missionaries and simply continued to take these problems to the "medicine man" as they had done before they came to Christ. We missionaries often decried their "bifurcated" Christianity but had no antidote.

We simply reproduced the secularized approach to illness and accident we had learned at home. We acted as though Western medicine was more effective than prayer. Oh, we prayed calmly for ordinary things and fervently when things got really bad, but medicine was our first choice, God our last. Without meaning to, we taught the people that the Christian God works only through Western medical techniques (though they soon learned that our medicine can't handle many of their needs). By observing Western doctors who were not Christian, however, they discovered that whatever power was available in our clinics was inherent in the medicine, not in the God we talked about. The God of power portrayed in the Scriptures seemed to have died.

Once the village medicine man began to attend church. His wife had died and some of the local Christians had so identified with him in his sorrow that he decided to check out Christianity. But he soon stopped attending. He probably found out that, though many of the sermons were about a miracle worker, the local Christians had none of that power themselves. In fact, when they needed healing, they would usually come to him (often even after they had tried Western medicine and found little or no relief from it). So he saw no point in joining the new movement.

Such experiences from my own days on the mission field lingered in my memory as I completed graduate school, taught at two secular universities, and eventually became a part of the Fuller faculty (in 1969). In this position, then, I began to receive two other nudges in the direction of openness to learning more about spiritual power. First, as we discussed the church worldwide, it became very obvious that the most rapid growth was taking place among Pentecostal and charismatic churches. I easily concurred with my colleagues that the reason was their relevance to people's interest in obtaining greater spiritual power, but I had no first-hand understanding of what this might mean.

The second thing that happened was that, as our student body grew, more and more Pentecostals and charismatics began to come to Fuller. I had seen some of the television personalities from this camp and had been quite put off by them. It was not, therefore, easy at first to overcome my stereotypes and to accept them as "normal" people. Yet a combination of exposure to people with this perspective and the knowledge that God was really working through them around the world led me to greater and greater openness to them as persons and to their points of view with regard to ministry.

It is interesting now to thumb through my book *Christianity in Culture* (written between 1973 and 1979), noting there a substantial number of statements that both indicate my changing perspective and lay a foundation for what has happened to me during the last five years. I allude several times to such things as the importance of the spirit world to most peoples, the inadequacy and partialness of any presentation of Christianity that does not address healing and deliverance, the fact that for most of the peoples of the world healing is a theological problem not simply a technological one, and the greater effectiveness of Pentecostal Christianity. Such statements have taken on new meaning for me now.

Additionally, I had gotten to know John Wimber. We met on several occasions between 1975 and 1977 while he was working with my colleague Peter Wagner in what was then known as the Fuller Evangelistic Association. I came to respect John as a church growth analyst. At that time he was not into a healing ministry and was even skeptical of the degree of openness we on the School of World Mission faculty had to the miraculous. I remember wondering what had happened to him to cause him to leave Fuller Evangelistic Association to start a church with a focus on healing.

My Paradigm Shift

Then came January 1982. Wagner had been in regular contact with Wimber between 1977 and 1982 and had kept up to some extent with the changes in his thinking and ministry. I had not. For me (and Meg) this was to be an adventure into a realm ordinarily populated by those I had stereotyped as "nonintellectual, hyperemotional, and often just plain weird." But we had known and learned to trust Wimber before he got "this way." So we came, we listened, and we observed.

There were over eighty students there each Monday evening. But even so, a senior professor had no place to hide—I was very visible. So I wanted to move cautiously. Yet the lectures were so convincing, the perspective so compatible with the direction in which I was groping, and the demonstrations (the healings) so hard to ignore, that I soon lost my reserve—except in the area of practice. I rather quickly became convinced that this was the direction in which I wanted to move—so much so that by about the fourth or fifth session, John asked me to do the lecture on worldviews, focusing on the shift that was taking place in my own Christian paradigm.

The struggle for me was not, however, at that level. As I sat there week after week, the intellectual material made lots of sense. It filled gaps in my thinking and experience I had wanted very much to fill. I had long since abandoned my early dispensationalist training and come to see Jesus as "the same yesterday, today and forever" (Heb. 13:8). If this is true, I expected miracles today as well as yesterday. But to this point, I had only heard that they were still occurring. I could not recall ever having seen something that I could confidently and unambiguously call a miracle. The course provided experiences to confirm and fill out my thinking.

The "words of knowledge" were a bigger intellectual challenge, yet I had already concluded that a living God is a still-revealing God. So these contemporary revelations fit into an experience gap that I had already allowed for. Yet they challenged my habit of behaving as if God does not reveal things today. To believe it is one thing; to see and hear it happening is quite another.

But the greatest challenge was to my own Christian practice, for Wimber taught that we are all to minister healing to others and that we should take advantage of this class setting to begin practicing such a ministry. He would not let us simply intellectualize about healing. He demonstrated, then told us to do likewise.

This was scary! I remember sitting in my seat, trembling as John would say, "If anyone near you stands up [for prayer], you lay hands on him or her and pray for him or her." I would literally ask God not to let anyone near me stand up! I was afraid it wouldn't work if I was involved. Perhaps I didn't "have the gift" or, worse yet, was too sinful for God to use me in this way—and I certainly didn't want to prejudice anyone's chances of getting healed by attempting to participate if my presence would block God's blessing. And besides that, I as a professor was so visible in the class that everyone would know I was a failure. Sometimes when someone near me did stand, I would smile as if I really knew what to do but stand and back off to watch the students deal with the situation.

Seeing people healed was so exciting, however, that I couldn't stop talking about it. The trouble, of course, was that this led others to assume that I knew how to do it. So I kept getting asked to pray for people—both in and out of class. And I did pray for them. But not much happened in 1982 and 1983. I was able to attend about half of the sessions of the Signs and Wonders course in 1983 (when the enrollment reached three hundred). I would also visit the Anaheim Vineyard from time to time. All of this served to confirm my change of attitude (my "paradigm shift") and to push me closer to what I call my "practice shift."

My Practice Shift

In early February 1984 the pastor of the church I belong to, Pasadena Covenant Church, announced a change to a Vineyard type format for the evening services. He asked me to be in charge of the prayer room. Though people did not come in large numbers, I got to pray with someone nearly every week. This gave me a bit of practice and enough happened to give me some confidence. I also began to be invited to Sunday school classes to teach on healing. I did this at first without seeking to actually pray for anyone. But as time went on and I developed more boldness, I began to seek opportunities to demonstrate what I was talking about in front of the class.

I was also able to attend most of the sessions of the healing seminar offered at Anaheim that month. A couple of things that proved to be very important to me happened at that seminar. Perhaps the most important was that I finally responded to God's prodding to deal with an area of sin in my life. For several months I had been pondering in amazement the way God had started to use me even before I dealt with this issue. I had assumed he only used people who had already taken care of such things. But he broke me down by starting to give me the desire of my heart (to be used in a healing ministry) even before I got right with him! I still can hardly believe his mercy. I just had to respond in gratefulness by getting rid of the sin. Then, a day or so after that event, God led the person sitting in front of me in one of the meetings to turn and speak a prophecy, the significance of which he could not have known. In that way God provided both confirmation that his hand was on me and powerful encouragement to continue in the direction in which I was moving.

In March 1984 I began to experience some pressure around my heart and was put in the hospital for three days of tests. The tests turned up a slight irregularity in my heartbeat at high levels of activity (on the treadmill). I was released but scheduled for another treadmill test the following week, after which a dye would be injected into my bloodstream to enable the doctors to view the heart on a television screen. This would enable them to determine if there was any blockage in the blood vessels serving my heart. I attended the healing class the following Monday evening and was prayed over for this condition and the blockage the doctors expected to find was not there! I rejoiced and pledged to God that I would henceforth seek to be a more active channel of this kind of blessing for others.

May was another pivotal month. I had been invited to speak at a weekend retreat for Christian college students. In discussions with the organizers, I found that several of them had had some kind of charismatic experience. I, therefore, shared freely with them my recent experiences. On Saturday morning, then, one of the music leaders turned up with a congested chest asking if I would pray for her. Several of us did and she got well immediately.

That afternoon another girl was badly hurt in a softball game. I was chatting with a group of students on a hillside when one of the group came running up the hill to me with the message, "Louann would like you to come pray for her." With little faith but lots of hope I went to her, laid my hand on her injured shoulder (she flinched in pain) and (along with one of the girls) prayed for her. Nothing happened. So they put a support under her neck, carefully moved her into a waiting station wagon and took her to a hospital. We went about our business, had our evening meal, and started the evening meeting.

As I started my message, in walked Louann with not so much as a bandage on her. The story she told was this: the ride to the hospital, she said, was the most painful thing she had ever experienced. The doctor took one look at her and ordered her neck X-rayed. The X-ray showed nothing. So he had her shoulder X-rayed. Nothing. Collarbone. Nothing. And as they were finishing that one, Louann looked up and said, "The pain's gone!" The doctor said something like, "I've been around long enough to know when someone is badly hurt. You were badly hurt. But the X-rays show nothing and you say the pain is gone. I can't explain it, but you might as well go home."

These experiences led me to the point where I said to the Lord, "I don't care even if you let me be embarrassed. I'm going to pray for anyone who wants to be prayed for. From now on, I'm going to be active rather than passive." It was this change of attitude that I point to as my "practice shift."

What I've Been Learning

By this time I've experienced many good things, both in this country and abroad, plus an additional healing of my own (from a kidney stone). I haven't seen any blind gain their sight or any crippled people jump and walk—yet. But there are many whom God has blessed by healing problems of the spine, stomach, shoulders, knees, and head or by lengthening a leg that was short. God has also allowed me to set many free from demons (usually minor ones so far) and from spiritual problems such as bitterness, worry, unforgiveness, anger, and the like.

I've been learning that *what we're about is ministry, not simply healing, ministry to the whole person.* Typically, we are asked to pray for some physical, psychological, or spiritual problem. But our calling is to be the vehicle of God's ministry to the whole person. And often God has something in mind quite different from what the person or the one who prays is focused on. On several occasions I have been addressing myself to a physical problem only to note that the person has been reduced to tears by God as he deals with something deeper and more important in the person's life. I prayed over a broken leg one time and God spoke to the man about his bitterness. I prayed that God would release a young woman from her crippledness and God began, in her words, to "clean me up inside." I prayed for the crippled legs of a woman who had been a victim of polio early in her life and God seemed to do nothing, but the woman considers that time of ministry to be the "high point of her spiritual life."

In one case, a woman had an arm that had gone numb on her. God led me to send from her spirits of fear and worry, and the arm was immediately better. In another case, a man had a knotted up muscle just above his left shoulder. The banishing of a spirit of inadequacy turned the muscle soft. In another case, a man requested prayer for a problem with his knees. Discovering that one of his legs was short, I commanded it to lengthen. When nothing happened after the third command, the Lord led me to ask if he was anxious about something. He was, we dealt with the problem, his leg was lengthening without further attention given to it, and God healed his knees.

I believe Jesus wants *everyone to minister to people by praying for their healing.* The disciples were empowered and commanded to minister in this way (Luke 9:1, 2) and later told to teach everything they had been taught (Matt. 28:20). Praying for healing is, therefore, more a matter of obedience than of gifting.

Not everyone we pray for gets healed. In fact, my average over the whole range of people and problems I deal with is probably less than 50 percent, if we are speaking of total healing of the condition for which we pray. If, however, we evaluate what happens in terms of ministry to the needy person, I find almost everyone experiences some significant and meaningful experience with God, whether or not the problem condition in focus is taken completely away. Several of the above illustrations highlight this fact.

I believe *there is a difference between praying and taking authority.* In Luke 9:1 we read that Jesus gave the disciples "power and authority to drive out all demons and to cure diseases." There is, of course, an important place for prayer; nothing gets done without it. But the prayer comes primarily in preparation for the ministry. In prayer we assure both God and ourselves that it is his will, not ours, that we desire. In prayer we ask for God to minister to the person who seeks his help. In prayer we confess our unworthiness and ask for his power to defeat the enemy in the coming encounter. Without prayer we have no authority and power. But in the encounter itself, whether for healing or deliverance, we are not to pray—we are to command. We work in the authority given to us over all demons and diseases. So we take the authority given us by Jesus over whatever the problem is and command it in Jesus' name to be resolved. At this point we are not praying to God to resolve the problem, but working as his agents, with his full authority to rearrange things in the spiritual realm.

Taking authority is most obvious in deliverance. We are to command demons to leave. But even in healing, we are to take authority over the disease or body part and command it to be well, even as Jesus did when "he ordered the fever to leave her" (Luke 4:39) or when he said to the leper "be clean" (Luke 5:13). We are to take authority also in blessing, cursing, and even forgiving (John 20:23). I regularly use formulas such as, "I bless you in Jesus' name," or "In Jesus' name I minister to you peace [or forgiveness, or confidence, or release from worry, fear, or guilt]." Often, then, God gives the recipient concrete feelings to go along with the blessing. But whether he or she feels anything or not, transactions take place in the spiritual realm when we assert the authority Jesus has given us.

One of the things that surprised me in this whole experience is that *we need to learn and experiment.* I had always assumed that people received the "gift" of healing (and probably other gifts as well) all at once. What I experience is a gradual learning process that comes along with constant practice and a lot of risk taking. The learning seems to center in at least three areas: ministering to people, listening to God, and developing greater faith and confidence to risk doing what one thinks one hears from God. The fear of being wrong is a powerful impediment, but God seems to bless more when we launch out in faith in spite of our fear and then when we make mistakes, pick ourselves up, and try again.

Overall, I treasure such lessons as the following: that I should try to minister healing even though frightened, lacking in faith, or even skeptical; that "even I" can do it; that God often blesses my attempts; that God does show me things through words of knowledge; that my "success" rate increases with practice; that even "faithing" is learned through experience; that God richly blesses both the one who prays and the one prayed for; that even when the person prayed for is not healed, God often ministers to him or her; that even after much experience there is still much to learn; and that even after seeing God do numerous exciting things, one may still find oneself skeptical from time to time!

Concluding Remarks

I am one of the many who have been profoundly affected through the ministry of John Wimber. God has used him to lead me into the most earthshaking and satisfying experience of my life. Not that I was dissatisfied—I have found my forty-two years of Christian experience very satisfying and rewarding, so I never dreamed it could be any better. Yet now I feel as if I've moved to an entirely new plane, where all of the things I have believed for these many years have taken on new life.

I find myself reading the Bible (especially the Gospels) with new eyes—knowing that angels and demons and miracles and deliverances and revelations from God and all those things I used to read about only as inspired history are for us today! I find a new desire to pray, to talk to God, and to listen to him. I experience a new boldness in speaking about my faith, a new confidence that God is in fact who I have long believed him to be. There is new power and authority in my ministry, as well as a compelling desire to minister to others. The fruits of the Spirit (Gal. 5:22, 23) are easier to practice. Tears of compassion are frequently in my eyes.

I am still pitifully human, as my wife can testify. But there are enough changes that it seems clear that nothing short of the power of God is at work in me. And I like it a lot! The words of one verse of the hymn "Loved With Everlasting Love" keep coming to mind:

Heaven above is softer blue,
Earth around is sweeter green.
Something lives in every hue,
Christless eyes have never seen.
Birds with gladder songs o'erflow,
Flowers with deeper beauty shine;

Since I know as now I know,
I am His and He is mine.

Could this be what the kingdom is intended to be? I believe God expects us to see with kingdom eyes, to live as kingdom people, to minister with kingdom power and authority. When we do, I believe we experience a new level of normalcy—what I like to call "kingdom normalcy." In the kingdom of God, things we refer to as miracles are the order of the day.

In the kingdom we can expect healings, deliverances, words of knowledge, angelic protection, food being multiplied, and weather being changed, as well as people being saved, loving the unlovable, forgiving the guilty, refusing to worry or take revenge or seek worldly prestige and power. I've always considered the last part of this list as normative for Christians. Coming to experience the first part of the list as well, however, puts the whole scriptural package together in an exciting way—in my life as well as in history. I like the "new" normalcy so much I never want to go back to the old.

6

Young Lady, Old Hag

John White

John White is an author, psychiatrist, and former missionary in Latin America. Currently he is serving as copastor of the Vineyard Christian Fellowship of North Delta, British Columbia. Born in England, he studied medicine in Manchester. He and his wife, Lorrie, have five grown children and three grandchildren.

I first saw the drawing in a psychology text. If I had seen it in a kid's magazine I would have been intrigued by just another visual trick. In a psychology text I was supposed to take it more seriously. Later, John Wimber featured it in the "Signs and Wonders" course at Fuller Seminary. Every time I looked at it I saw this hideous old woman, evil-eyed and hook-nosed. I saw what I was conditioned to see, what my *mental set* was predisposed to see. Then suddenly she would vanish and in her place would be a sweet young thing looking coyly away from me over a fur draped on her left shoulder.

I could never see both of them at once; I had to be content with one woman or the other. The old woman was the easiest for me to conjure up. Indeed she would be there immediately whenever I looked at the drawing. If I wanted to see the girl I had to do a paradigm shift to conjure her up. It became a sort of game to see first one, then the other, then the first again.

Only at times I wasn't sure who was playing the game. Was I in control? Or were they? The two of them seemed to be battling for my attention, so that now one, now the other would dominate the state of

my consciousness. In fact it's still like that. The battle is not over, but at present the sweet young thing is winning.

It was the same in real life. I didn't have one paradigm shift but many, seeing the world now one way, now another. I did not realize what was happening to me, but I bumbled through my Christian life puzzled and confused by what seemed to be happening inside me. From the dispensational teaching of my youth I gathered that life was now largely nonsupernatural. And (though my teachers never intended this) I saw the life of Jesus as largely irrelevant—what mattered was his death.

Yet I felt cheated. There was something powerfully attractive about the synoptic Gospels. Deep called to deep as I read them. I wanted the Jesus I glimpsed there, but (though nobody actually said so) he was forbidden territory. He had been there for the Jews, and they had refused him. It seemed manifestly unfair that I didn't get a crack at that Jesus too. I learned all about substitutionary atonement, and I gratefully accepted the Savior in my heart and with my will.

But I wanted the whole of him—not just his dying love, but his earthly living.

Medical Studies

But even then there were glimpses of his working in our world today. I remember my mother looking at me startled one day. "John," she said, "your Auntie Jennie must be having an operation. I can smell the chloroform. We must pray!" She didn't normally talk like that and was not subject to whims or fancies. And she had never heard of "words of knowledge." So we prayed. And it turned out that Auntie Jennie *was* having an emergency operation right then and made a good recovery.

Again and again over the years I caught a glimpse of a different world, a world where the supernatural was part of everyday life and not merely relegated to my own "spiritual" battles. Only glimpses. They never stayed. After all, I never expected them to, wondering afterward whether they had really happened. Once when I was in my second year of medical studies, our family doctor told us there was no hope for my mother. She would die soon of heart failure and hospitalization was uncalled for. She would die at home; he was no longer able to save her.

My medical studies had confirmed my early religious training. Life was governed by material laws. God intervened nowadays only in the conversion and sanctification of sinners and in supplying the material needs of missionaries, but it was permitted to pray for his intercession anyway. And as I prayed I asked God what I was supposed to pray *for*. Was there any point in asking him to heal my mother after what the doctor had said?

Don't ask me how God spoke to me, but he did. He told me to ask for her healing. And whenever over the next week or two I had fantasies about being at my mother's funeral playing the role of the bereaved and grieving son, the Holy Spirit would rebuke me. "Don't indulge in this kind of fantasy if you ask for your mother's healing."

Then one night as I took her medication to her she could not speak properly. She whispered, "I can't breathe. There's a weight on my chest. If only I could sleep . . ." I gave her the medication and went into the next bedroom. It was dark and cold, and I didn't bother to switch the light on. I knelt down and said, "God, if you're going to do anything, you'd better do it now!" There was nothing else to say. After a minute or two I got up off my knees and went to my mother's room.

As I came through the door I was startled to hear her speak in her normal voice. "You've just been praying, haven't you?" she said. "And God is answering your prayer." She was up and about a week later and lived for forty years after that, free of any heart disease. I assumed that a sovereign God must occasionally break the dispensational rules, but I was careful not to presume on his grace. I didn't ask him for any more healings.

Loretta O'Hara

At least not until I got into the New Tribes Mission. By then I had completed medical studies and had begun surgical residencies. I interrupted the surgical residencies to take missionary training, feeling it would be wise to take language and linguistic studies before I got too old to learn new languages. On my way to the New Tribes boot camp in Pennsylvania I was praying in the corridor of the train. Suddenly I *knew* I would meet my future wife at the boot camp. It was a profound knowing. Marriage had been the last thing in my mind as I had prayed, yet I knew. And like my mother, I had never heard of words of knowledge. However, when I looked the girls over at the boot camp, I pushed my "knowing" to the back of my mind. There was no way I was going to marry any of them.

Almost a year later I was taking part in the early morning prayer meeting when something unusual happened to me. That morning my folder with the latest correspondence from a missionary overseas contained a letter from a Loretta O'Hara in the Philippines. She was in the American hospital in Manila seriously ill. Evidently the diagnosis was not clear: either she was suffering from carcinoma in her cervical spine or else the vertebrae were invaded by tuberculosis.

I could not understand what was happening to me as I read the letter. I was disturbed and angry. I heard myself demanding that God put an end to the situation right away. I was shocked by the expressions coming out of my mouth, but they came anyway. I didn't know who she was, but she *had to recover from it*. God had to answer my prayers.

Not long after, Loretta O'Hara came through the boot camp on her way back to the Philippines. She was a stunningly attractive girl, black-haired, slender, a little defiant, and she told me her side of the story. The letter I read was out of date. She was already back in Canada when I had prayed. The diagnosis had been confirmed both in the Philippines and in Canada as tuberculosis of the cervical spine. On the day I had prayed she had been on her way to a tuberculosis sanatorium and had to break her journey in Halifax, Nova Scotia. At first she had turned down an urgent request to speak at a young people's rally there. But later that day, feeling she should do so, she agreed to preach from an armchair; she was in too much pain to stand.

Yet as she looked at the congregation, she knew that she could not preach sitting down. So she struggled to her feet, clutched the reading desk, and started. And as she spoke, she became aware that a miracle was taking place in her body. She was being healed.

She never went to the sanatorium but returned home the next day. She asked her doctor for more X-rays. She wanted a new report that the mission would accept, so that she could return to the Philippines. Her doctor, who had struggled with red tape to get her the place in the sanatorium, was angry at what he saw as her stubbornness. But he repeated his X-rays and blood work and was bewildered to find there was no evidence of disease in her body. I have examined the reports personally and can vouch for the reality of the documentary evidence.

Loretta O'Hara did not return to the Philippines. We married and went to Latin America together, and it was there that all of our five children were born. But neither of us grasped the significance of what had taken place. The young girl with the fur draped over her left shoulder had ogled us both repeatedly, but we had failed to see her. Yes, God had acted miraculously, but his action, surely, was exceptional. And the reality of what God had done faded. It had happened, but it seemed to belong to another order of reality, not the reality we were living in. The paradigm shift (if there had been one) had taken place for a brief interim only.

A Humanist

The ugly face of the old woman still dominated the picture. One of our missionary friends developed a virulent form of cancer, with secondaries in her cervical spine. Some who prayed for her assured us that God had told them clearly that their prayers were answered. She would be healed; it was already done in heaven. But Lorrie and I had no such assurance. And as our friend died, we saw how great the danger was of misplaced faith. The old woman leered at us from the drawing.

Yet it kept happening. Suddenly the world would change for a brief instant. Twice the strange shift in perception was repeated. Once it concerned a woman friend who had been diagnosed as suffering from an incurable condition in her connective tissues. She was in pain and had felt sick for some months. The news disturbed me. We stood facing each other outside the Church of the Way, and I placed my hand on her shoulder and prayed. A picture of fibrous tissue invading muscles filled my mind, and indignantly I insisted that it not be so. Suddenly it seemed that I had the right to make such a demand. The paradigm had briefly shifted. She thanked me, and years later reported to me that she was fine. And she looked it. Yet as she spoke I sort of nodded to myself. "Her doctors must have been wrong," I thought. The old hag's face still haunted me.

Then there was the little girl with a malignant condition in her jaw. She faced removal of at least part of her lower jaw and its replacement by a metal prosthesis. I suddenly saw the world differently. Again I felt rage against evil and momentary triumph over it as I laid my hands on her (it was not a custom of mine) to pray the condition away. Yet later when I heard the tumor was encapsulated I thought, "I guess it must have been benign all along." The paradigm by means of which I constructed my world was not altogether stable, but it was basically humanist, even though I was a devout theist.

Demon Chasers

But before long it became clearer what was happening to me. It started with the issue of demons. I discovered that a few of my psychiatric patients in Winnipeg were demonized. I was reluctant to come to the conclusion, for demon chasers had always seemed a bunch of crazies to me. They made stupid claims that I knew were not true; I didn't want to join their number. Yet in some of my patients the evidence of demons became undeniable.

One woman was the organizing secretary of a Winnipeg gay organization. I had originally diagnosed her as suffering from bipolar affective illness. After her deliverance from demons she said to me one day, "Know what? I'm not a lesbian."

"Oh," I replied casually. "When did you decide to quit?"

"Decide nothing!" she said. "When the demons were gone, I wasn't!" And to this day she still isn't. Nor does she need any medication for her supposed mental illness.

But I knew that in some obscure way I was "flying blind." I was dealing with the supernatural, but I didn't know what I was doing. I was clumsily following rules. I was in touch with something I could neither see nor sense. I went to a symposium on demons organized by the Christian Medical Society at Notre Dame University, where Bible scholars, theologians, philosophers, and physicians wrestled with the problem of evil. I had been asked to present a paper there, but my real hope was to break through my own confusion.

I think most of the participants in the symposium were in the same condition I was myself. Among us we had a lot of knowledge and a certain amount of experience, but we groped for true understanding. The knowledge was valuable (the papers are printed in the book *Demon Possession,* published by Bethany Press). However, during a private conversation with a Christian anthropologist light began to dawn.

He had been working with a primitive tribe in East Africa. One day he had an interesting exchange with his native informant. "You must be very lonely," the informant told him.

"Oh? What makes you say so?" the anthropologist replied.

"Well, when I have a problem I talk to the spirit of my father, and the spirit of my grandfather, and they talk it over with the spirit of my great grandfather. Then they give me their advice. It comforts me."

"So what makes you think that I don't talk to the spirits of *my* father and my grandfather?"

"You don't. I can't see them. They're not around you."

As I listened the penny dropped. The identity of the spirits with which the informant conversed is neither here nor there; most Christians would say he was talking with demons. But I saw that a "primitive" East African retained an ability to perceive the spirit world, even though his perception was distorted and misleading. I had no such ability. Demons could be all round me in the hospital, yet I could only deduce their presence occasionally by a process of logic. I could not *perceive* them. Had I as a Westerner lost the capacity to perceive the supernatural, a capacity largely retained by non-Westerners?

I began to pray that God would restore it to me. I had no unnatural craving for esoteric experiences; it was just that I was fighting evil in my patients. I needed help in dealing with issues that transcended materiality.

From Ontario to Fuller

But I was soon to leave psychiatry. The demand for my writing and addresses had reached a point where either I would have to stop writing and preaching so as to concentrate on psychiatry and training psychiatrists, or else I would have to leave psychiatry. Lorrie and I prayed about it, and in the end we decided I should quit the profession. With relief I stopped asking God to restore my ability to perceive the supernatural; the gift would no longer be necessary. Or so I thought.

We retired to a lovely condominium on the shores of a lake in northwestern Ontario. I could walk through the woods or trudge in winter across the frozen lake. I could sense the Lord walking with me. Writing was going well, but something was missing. Somehow we were in a spiritual backwater. Gradually a craving built up inside me to be at the spiritual battlefront. I wanted to "die with my boots on," to be involved in hand-to-hand conflict.

One evening as we were talking, Lorrie told me she was experiencing the same yearning. Unknown to each other, we had each been praying separately about it for weeks. We began to pray together. Then from California, where he was working on his D.Min., Ken Blue called us. He had been with us at the Church of the Way in Winnipeg as associate minister. I would be interested in meeting John Wimber, Ken said. He had the same idea as I had about Westerners and the difficulty in perceiving the world the way Third World people found more natural. We decided to visit Fuller and enroll in Wimber's course. The seminary was kind enough to welcome me as a visiting scholar.

Fuller Seminary has three faculties, one of theology, another of psychology, plus a third, the School of World Mission. The last-named sponsors MC510, "Signs, Wonders and Church Growth." Dr. Peter Wagner is responsible for MC510. The course is given by John Wimber and is designed to explore the theology of the miraculous in evangelism and in church life and to teach students to experience spiritual gifts and to learn to heal.

Over 130 students attended the course in the winter quarter. Students varied greatly in age and denominational affiliation and while men predominated, a large number of women were present. About a third of the students were older men and an occasional woman from Third World countries; most had considerable pastoral experience. School of World Mission and theology students predominated; psychology majors were in a minority.

Attendance had to be monitored at the beginning of the course to keep nonregistered students out. Once the course was under way, attendance held up well. Most students seemed to come with open and friendly attitudes, and perhaps a mingling of desire to learn along with a healthy skepticism. As the course proceeded, the skepticism diminished progressively, so that the majority became actively involved in healing and attempted healing outside class time, often reporting enthusiastically their out-of-class experiences.

Classes were held in the basement of a church just off campus from 6 to 9 PM every Monday evening. They rarely ended on time, since many students were involved in discussion and prayer until they were more or less driven out of the room.

Manifestations

Two hours were devoted to didactic material along with questions and discussion and the third hour was a laboratory session. The laboratory session was designed to get students involved in putting what they learned into practice. Its form varied each week. During the laboratory sessions, "manifestations" of various kinds could be witnessed, though no attempt was made in the course to create or bring about such phenomena.

Students were encouraged, however, to observe what was happening when fellow students were experiencing an anointing of the Holy Spirit, so that they might learn to perceive what God was doing. During the second session, individuals all over the room could be observed sitting peacefully, their faces perspiring a little, many with eyes closed. Head and hands would often shake.

Roused from such a condition and questioned about what they experienced, students (many of whom were older men and women) would profess to be fully aware of their surroundings, give no explanation of their condition, but say they experienced joy, peace, and a sense of well-being. In some cases, the condition continued over days and weeks intermittently, but it did not hinder their studies or occupation. Gradually it would subside.

During the laboratories, healing would take place. It was impossible to assess and evaluate all that was going on, in that toward the end of the course so many things would be taking place at once that it would have taken twenty or thirty observers to record everything. Small groups would fill the room, each attempting to minister to one of their number.

However, a few of the healings were dramatic and did not admit of any "psychological" or psychosomatic mechanism known to me personally. The third laboratory was introduced by John Wimber inviting five or six people who wanted healing to come to the front of and to face the class. Promptly five members came forward, and a sixth came limping on a single crutch.

Wimber then quietly prayed a one-sentence prayer requesting that the Holy Spirit manifest himself in whatever way he chose to do so. After praying, Wimber sat down in the front row, and two men from his church who had experience in healing began to interview two of the students who were facing the rest of the class. Their conversation was inaudible to the rest of us.

Wimber quietly drew our attention to the man with the crutch who was standing at one end of the line. "Notice his face and eyes," he said, adding quietly, "I won't say anything more in case I either influence what you see or impart suggestions to him."

The young man's face was uplifted and shining with perspiration. His eyelids were fluttering. Gradually his head and upper arms began to tremble, at first gently, then with increased violence. Soon his whole body was shaking and to such an extent that it seemed he would lose his balance and fall. His crutch crashed to the floor and one or two students came forward to lay the man gently on the ground, where his shaking became ever more violent.

The shaking somewhat resembled one of the phases of a grand mal seizure but differed in that it was less coordinated and did not follow the regular sequence of grand mal. Nor did it reflect any other form of epilepsy I have ever seen. By now, the young man's right leg was flailing in every direction, kicking someone's briefcase across the floor. I was concerned to see his left leg (which I had mistakenly taken to be the injured leg) lying doubled beneath the leg that flailed and called to the class members nearest to him to release the leg gently. When they attempted to do so they seemed to become involved in the shaking themselves, so that they were unable to follow my direction.

After about five to seven minutes the whole thing subsided and the young man was helped to his feet and the crutch handed back to him. Wimber approached him with the microphone and asked him whether he was aware of all that had been happening to him. He said he was. Could he describe his experience?

The young man told us he was a football player with a ruptured Achilles tendon. The tendon had been sutured, the foot immobilized in a cast for a month or so, and the cast removed two days before. He was undergoing physiotherapy, had as yet almost no movement in the foot (a small amount of dorsiflexion), and a certain amount of pain. He had felt a little disappointed when the shaking began, since it was initially confined to his arms. He stared at his foot. "I wish I had measured the exact amount of movement in it before this happened," he said.

"How much movement do you have now?" Wimber asked. The man was leaning against the wall and flexed his foot upwards. It was then I realized that the flailing foot had been the injured one. Had I known it at the time, I would have been alarmed, expecting the tendon (which is very slow in healing) to rupture again as the stitches tore out.

"How does that compare with the movement in the other foot?" Wimber asked. The left foot was raised. We all saw that it paralleled the right foot exactly. Its owner stared at it unbelievingly.

"What about movement in other directions?" Wimber asked.

"Nothing."

"And now?"

Tentatively at first, then with increasing confidence, the young man moved his foot in all directions. Clearly he enjoyed a full range of movement. Cautiously, he placed the injured foot on the floor and tried putting weight on it. "There's still a little pain," he said.

By now he was taking a few steps. But the class's attention began to be focused on other matters. A little self-consciously the young man placed the crutch under his arm and walked back to his place. The following week he testified that he had "not really believed he was healed" until about Wednesday (the second day following class) when he had given away his crutch. Further physiotherapy was discontinued by his doctor, who was puzzled and urged caution. The young man was jubilant.

Not a Tame Lion

I cannot even describe all that I saw or affirm a supernatural healing in every case (though I have no doubt of direct divine intervention in the case of the young man with the ruptured tendon). Some healings were instantaneous and attended by no dramatic manifestations. Others were real but progressive, that is to say, healing took place in stages during several prayer sessions. Sometimes healing would not happen during a prayer session, only to follow during the hours and days succeeding the session. At other times, no healing would take place at all. Sometimes the healing could have been explained on a psychological basis, that is, it was similar to healings carried out using hypnosis or suggestion. At other times no such explanation would suffice.

The reactions of individual class members to all that was taking place varied. Some members were initially disturbed and a few frightened; others were filled with enthusiasm. Those who felt disturbed were allowed to express their objections freely and to ask whatever questions there was time for. No attempt was made to talk them into anything. Slowly over the weeks, the negative and fearful reactions subsided and a sense of reverence, awe, and quiet rejoicing became more characteristic of the class.

A few of the manifestations were frightening and involved the demonic, though their origin was not brought out in class. On one occasion, a foreign student began to howl with ever-increasing volume, to the dismay and the agitation of those who were in prayer for him. I observed John Wimber move quietly behind him, touch him, and murmur, "Be at peace!" Immediately the hubbub was silenced.

On another occasion, a student began to speak in tongues, again in ongoing crescendo, which drew ever more attention to him. Once more, John Wimber touched him as he passed by, saying quietly, "Be at peace!" At once, the noise stopped, and the man was indeed at peace.

I have no clear understanding of the manifestations I observed during the course. What has shaking got to do with holiness? I don't know. However, I accept Jonathan Edwards's view that movements of the Spirit of God may be associated with manifestations that make no particular sense to me, and that while some may be harmful, others are at the worst harmless, and some positively beneficial. A sovereign God may not fit in with contemporary evangelical views of propriety. Aslan is not a tame lion.

Asia

For some people a paradigm shift comes easily, but not for most of us in Western culture. What we learned at Fuller is that to experience a paradigm shift you have to act consistently as if the universe corresponds to the view the Bible gives us of it. That's rough, although in moments of enthusiasm it's relatively easy. In fact, it can be a heady experience, "fun," as John Wimber would put it.

Not long after our three months in California we were scheduled for three months of meetings in Japan, Malaysia, Singapore, Hong Kong, and mainland China, all at the invitation of Asian Christians. At times the pace was killing. In Malaysia we were beyond exhaustion. Often there were long lines of people waiting to see us both before and after the meetings. Yet how could we hold ourselves back from the large crowds of yearning people? For once we had power to deliver the fearful, the demonized, and the sick.

Two incidents stand out in my mind. One concerned a Chinese girl, a shriveled, terrified little thing of twenty or so. Her eyes were big with terror. She lived with an aunt whose house was full of idols; there was no place else for her to go. She told us she dared not look at the idols, which oppressed and haunted her. She could not sleep and was crippled by her fears. We prayed with her, rebuking with authority the spirits that molested her. Then we told her to go back to her aunt's house, stand before every idol, look at it squarely, and say, "He that is in me is mightier than he who is in you."

We did not recognize her when she came the next night—neither of us could believe it was the same girl. She stood erect, her face was full of laughter, and she appeared totally free from fear. She gloried in the mighty Deliverer who dwelt within her own being.

The other was a little girl of around two years old. Her body was almost covered with eczematous eruptions; many areas were open and weeping but others were dry, angry, and red. Her parents were haggard. She had kept them awake for the previous thirty-six hours. They had to catch her to bring her to us for prayer, and she struggled as they brought her. Yet the moment we laid our hands on her she fell instantly into a profound and relaxed sleep. And as we prayed for about twenty-five minutes we were stunned to observe the weeping areas visibly shrinking in size and the redness fading in the dry areas. She woke before we could finish praying, but when they brought her back a couple of days later, there was no sign of the eczema.

An Inauspicious Beginning

In Canada we wanted to teach others what we had learned, but teaching would have to be more than verbal instruction. It would have to involve demonstrations and practical directions. We were novices ourselves. Often when we prayed, nothing happened, though always people seemed grateful and blessed. But what if we had a public demonstration and nothing happened? How would people learn? And what kind of fools would we look like?

At a Christian camp we were encouraged to try a public demonstration. Curiosity was aroused, and even the skeptics stayed. We asked for volunteers who would not mind us asking questions in public. The first young woman who came up had a severe skin condition. We prayed—but nothing happened. The second likewise had had eczema all her life and was also asthmatic. The moment we laid our hands on her she had a severe asthmatic attack and gasped, "I can't breathe."

It was an inauspicious beginning of a demonstration of healing. Dismay and fear seemed to flood the watchers. Without thinking what I was doing I raised my hand and commanded the attack to go. It did—immediately. And as we went on praying, her eczema was healed.

From that point on the demonstration was clear sailing. And a year later the asthmatic girl told us that for the first time she had had a year free of allergies, eczema, and asthma. Curiously, the first girl also came to us a year later. Following our unsuccessful attempt to heal her skin condition she had had a dream in which the Lord appeared to her and told her that a demon had been cast out as we prayed. From that point on the incessant quarrels that had severely threatened her marriage and her husband's pastoral ministry had come to an end. But she still had her skin condition.

How did all this make us feel? True, we had had more failures than successes in praying for the sick, but there had been plenty of successes, many more than we could describe in a book, and some of them pretty dramatic. Many had had to do with deliverance from sin and transformed marriages. As a psychiatrist I had been instrumental in helping many marriages, but now the Holy Spirit would sometimes fall on people as we prayed, and lifelong problems would be sorted out in a relatively short time. And the changes proved stable as months and years passed.

God Is Faithful

Did we exult? A little, but rather tentatively. Lorrie was more matter-of-fact about it all than I was. I am a doubter by nature; I have to have everything tied down. Were we now confident? Not altogether. Sometimes we found ourselves describing to other people some marvelous answer to prayer or other. But half the time we were doing so to convince ourselves that the event had really happened, for, strangely, even when we saw miracles take place under our own eyes, we had a job grasping that what we saw was reality or that God had really used us. Seeing is not always believing. And it helped our faith less than you might suppose. Something that is deliriously exciting on Monday may seem unreal and remote by Wednesday.

And after four months of ministry in another country where we encountered a great deal of skepticism, we felt more like licking our wounds than exulting. We had encountered so many failures and so few successes there that we felt like giving up.

But God was faithful to us. What we had learned as a result of a crisis, he patiently drilled us in everyday practice. The learning is endless, and for me that constituted a special difficulty. You acquire a certain attitude toward learning in universities, not necessarily the best attitude—learn that you have to master, to dominate each new area that confronts you. In my case it had been an endless process, and one I had grown weary of. I had twelve years of formal university training, and as a researcher and professor I had to continue the endless process of acquiring more knowledge, keeping up with ever-increasing literature and the acquiring of new skills. This is particularly true of medicine, where rapidly advancing knowledge calls for rapidly changing techniques. As one grows older one becomes less adaptable. Inwardly it had all become burdensome. "Of making of many books there is no end, and much study wearies the body," said the Preacher (Eccles. 12:12). My body was good and weary.

So, faced with new learning I groaned. I had not bargained for it. But it is a different kind of learning and infinitely less burdensome. I had the wrong picture in mind. I felt I would have to *master* this new thing, just as I had been obliged to dominate everything I had tackled in life. And I had my fill of new worlds to conquer. So when John Wimber had challenged us at Fuller, I groaned inwardly. Would it never end? Would I have to acquire new learning until I died?

Yes and no—but mostly no. His yoke is proving to be easy, his burden light. It refreshes the body more than it wearies it. For me it has been a continuation of a kind of learning that has been going on steadily all my life, a going further along the same familiar biblical pathway, of walking with the Lord, of meditating on the written word and seeking the Living Word. I am still learning to be more sensitive to the Holy Spirit, but curiously, in some odd and indefinable way, this has been a moving into home territory. There is familiarity and assurance, as I recognize that I am not moving into new territory at all. It seemed like new territory at first, but now, as the mists clear, I find I am in the same country I have loved so long and dearly.

And I am beginning to relax. I don't have to learn everything in a day. I don't have to prove anything—not my manhood, nor my intelligence, nor even my spirituality. I just have to go on discovering who it is who loves me so much, wants to commune with me so much (he alone knows why), and how to respond to him. I have little responsibility—just to trust him and obey. His commandments are not burdensome.

III

Doctrinal Encounters

When theological convictions fail to answer pressing questions about how to live the Christian life, conflict follows. Sometimes we are not aware of a theological system's deficiencies until we have a crisis that points them out. In other instances a crisis is brought on after years of little failures that erode our confidence. Under these circumstances the crisis may be long in coming, but it hits like a slap in the face. Then we say, "Maybe something I have never questioned needs to be examined more closely. Perhaps I have been wrong." That's what each person in this section did, and because these people trusted God and submitted to Scripture when they did it, he blessed them greatly.

7

Not Now, but Later

George Mallone

George Mallone is pastor of Grace Vineyard, Arlington, Texas. He recently served as pastor of Burnaby Christian Fellowship, Burnaby, Canada, and for sixteen years was a pastor in the Vancouver area. He has written three books, and he and his wife, Bonnie, have three children.

On November 5, 1964, "Landslide" Lyndon Johnson was elected president of the United States. As a Texan I should have found cause for much festivity in my university dormitory, but that night was full of contradictory feelings. Two days prior my newly born-again girlfriend had given me a copy of *Living Letters*. This precursor to the *Living Bible* began with Paul's Letter to the Romans and this was my first real exposure to the New Testament. A few hours past midnight, not able to sleep, I settled down once again to read. In a matter of minutes I was overwhelmed by Romans 6:23 and, kneeling on the floor, I asked God for his "free gift." This revelation of a new life was instantaneous. I knew that I had been transformed, that God had his hand on my life, and that I must follow his direction and not my own. By morning light I was packing my car, leaving the university, and heading home to my family in Dallas. I knew I had changed and that I could not stay in my present environment without losing what was now so dear.

"I Fight Christians Anywhere"

Within a few days I was directed to a "good fundamental church," which became home for the next four years. Reinhardt Bible Church belonged to the Independent Fundamental Churches of America (IFCA) or what some of us jokingly called "I Fight Christians Anywhere." Reinhardt was a solid Bible teaching church with a dispensational framework. Two of Dallas Theological Seminary's outstanding professors were members of the congregation and frequent contributors. Dr. John F. Walvoord was the seminary's president and spokesman for pneumatology. Dr. Merrill F. Unger was Professor of Old Testament and author of the well received *Unger's Bible Dictionary* and *Biblical Demonology*. He was also an outspoken proponent of the theory of the cessation of miraculous gifts.

I will always be indebted to the excellent teaching and discipleship I received in that church. I was taught the inspiration and authority of God's Word, the inductive method of Bible study, and creative means for communicating that Word. This instruction has proven to be a stable mooring in my life and the direction of my ministry.

Shortly after my conversion, I enrolled in Dallas Bible College, where I took one semester of training. The semester proved a blessing, as I was given a doctrinal foundation for my faith. But it was also a hindrance, because it took me years to get over the narrow perspective of the Holy Spirit taught there. It was solid teaching, but it was limited in its exegetical insight and cautious in its emotional response to the Holy Spirit.

Inter-Varsity Christian Fellowship

In the fall of 1965 I returned to my former university and with the help of several friends launched a chapter of Inter-Varsity Christian Fellowship. Three years later I married an IVCF worker, Bonnie Burns, and the two of us were sent to Houston for the next three years to pioneer new works for IVCF.

At this time we attended another independent church pastored by a scholarly and honest student of God's Word. Seldom, if ever, did he push anything on me; rather he always challenged me with another question from Scripture. I remember one important discussion over coffee in which I asked him frankly: "Ed, do the Scriptures teach that certain gifts of the Spirit ceased with the apostles?" His answer was another question, but the direct impression I received, although he did not say so, was the cessationist position could not be proven from the Scriptures. This interaction laid the first plank of doubt about my dispensational understanding of the Spirit.

Throughout my staff days with IVCF I came into contact with teachers whose backgrounds were broader than my dispensational one, but who were still in the same cessationist stream. I remember watching John Stott debate David Howard, then the Missions Director of IVCF, on the subject of the gifts of the Holy Spirit. Howard took the position that these gifts were available to the church and that he had seen their operation on the mission field. Stott responded graciously but straightforwardly that what happened in the New Testament was not necessarily the same that was happening today, another way of saying the gifts had ceased

Vancouver, Here We Come

In 1971 Bonnie and I left Houston for Vancouver, British Columbia, to enroll in a new graduate school called Regent College. Its faculty come mostly from the ranks of the Plymouth Brethren, an ecclesiastical tradition I eventually joined. This movement had strong cessationist roots that ran back to the dispensational godfather John Nelson Darby. My theological mentors in the movement, men like F. F. Bruce, James Houston, Carl Armerding, and Ward Gasque, were moderates in their responses to the gifts; thus I was given room to research and experiment within a climate of acceptance.

Shortly after my arrival in Vancouver, I was asked to speak on the campus of the University of British Columbia to the local IVCF group. In the rear of the auditorium sat an elderly man. Bob Birch was the first IVCF worker in Canada, being present when the name Inter-Varsity Christian Fellowship was chosen for the Canadian student work (1929). Bob watched my ministry with the students and invited me to speak the following Sunday evening at the lively congregation he pastored, St. Margaret's Church.

Feeling greatly honored by his invitation, I was aghast to discover that the church was "charismatic." At that time my theology and experience made me a "fire-breathing anti-Pentecostal and anticharismatic" and I could not imagine speaking in such a context. I went along to the meeting and quickly found myself moved by the worship and the friendliness with which I was received. From that point on I spent much time with Bob and never in our conversations did he ever once ask if I had been baptized in the Holy Spirit or if I had spoken in tongues. I remember saying to myself, "If he is a charismatic, he is the most unusual one I have ever met."

Several months later Bob invited me to a small luncheon with an Englishman named David Watson. I thought to myself, "Here comes the heavy! I'm sure this guy is really going to lay on the charismatic trip!" When David stood up to speak, he seemed like a reincarnation of John Stott. He sounded like Stott, he expounded the Scriptures like Stott, he even had his thumbs in his britches like Stott. This completely confused my program as to what "charismatics" believed and how they were to act. Leaving the meeting I said to myself, "I want to write that man and find out what makes him tick."

Evangelical Agnosticism

My writing to David was delayed, although I knew his address by heart, as I found myself immersed in congregational concerns at Marineview Chapel where I had become a teaching elder. One area was particularly stressful and I devoted much of a year praying for the resolution of that problem. The showdown came and it seemed obvious to me that God had not heard a word I prayed. So, by an act of my will, I chose to become an evangelical agnostic. I preached like a theist, but in real life I lived like a deist. I believed in the gospel, but

I no longer believed that God was actively present nor heard my prayers.

I persisted in this state for several months, but it was interrupted on a flight out of Los Angeles back to Vancouver after a summer holiday. My nine-month-old daughter, Faye, was suffering from an ear infection and the change in air pressure once the plane became airborne caused her to scream in pain. In desperation I cried out, "God I know you are not listening to my prayers, but if you will just put this child to sleep, I'll start believing and talking to you again." Before you could say "Kathryn Kuhlman," Faye was out like a light. I found this somewhat disturbing.

Help, There's a Charismatic in My Bedroom

When I returned from my holiday I discovered that some "charismatic" influence had been deposited in our church while I was away. Three decidedly crucial things happened at this point.

First, while I was lunching in the faculty lounge of the university, someone pointed out a new professor and said to me, "You know, Bob is from David Watson's church in York." Knowing that I had failed to write to David and thinking this man might be able to help, I made friends with Bob and his wife, Marilyn. In a short time God led them to our congregation and they began to model for us a sober yet powerful relationship with the Holy Spirit.

The second encouragement came from my own wife. As a good evangelical, Bonnie had sublimated many of her mystical desires in the reading of C. S. Lewis and J. R. R. Tolkien. Yet neither of these was able to meet the fullest need of her heart. One day while she was interceding for me, God suddenly released within her the very presence of his Spirit. There came a new freshness and vigor to her life and she spoke in a language she did not know. You can imagine my reaction, as a good "Brethren worker" who did not really believe these things were possible, when she told me what had happened. Suddenly our bedroom became a battlefield. Painfully we tried to reconcile what we had been taught with what was presently happening. This experience later taught me that every renewal in the Holy Spirit will automatically produce fear in others, no matter how gently it is handled.

The third crucial event was a question posed to me by one of the other elders. I had been teaching through Romans 5–8 when Mark approached me and said, "George, you keep telling us what you don't believe about the Spirit. Why don't you tell us what you do believe?" He nailed me and I knew it. The only teaching I knew on the Holy Spirit was essentially negative and I was at a loss to say anything positive.

This question plus Bonnie's experience put me on a one-year search. Every day I prayed that God would teach me about the Holy Spirit. I also began to read everything I could find on the subject, from classic works to newer testimonies. Many days I would spend the entire day in prayer asking God to fill me with his Spirit. For most of the year there was no obvious answer to my prayer. And then, a few little things began to happen. Dreams and visions began to occur. God even used some of these in the conversion of other people. I began to suspect that something significant was happening.

86 East Parade, York

When we had been with our congregation for three years, we were given a six-week sabbatical. I thought it was about time that I finally talked with David Watson. Our marriage had suffered enough strain in this search for the Spirit and it was time to resolve some of my own questions.

After arriving in York we had our first scheduled appointment with David. Sitting in his living room, Bonnie and I poured out stories of the past five years. His comment at the end was the most assuring word I had ever heard: "Congratulations, you have both been filled with the Holy Spirit!" Bonnie needed to hear from this reputable authority that even though my experience had been different from hers, even though mine was slow and spread out over a year, while hers was sudden and sensationally transforming, both of us had been filled with the same Holy Spirit.

With this assurance under our belts we spent the remaining time absorbing the dimensions of the Spirit transpiring at St. Michael's in York. There was worship, dance, and drama. There were prophecies and evangelistic outreach. There was so much more than I ever believed possible for the church.

"Not Now, but Later!"

Returning to Vancouver, we began to learn as much as we could about the gifts of the Holy Spirit. We began to exercise words of knowledge and prophecy as we prayed for people. Within a year, all alone in my study, I began speaking in tongues. It was such an unusual thing for me that I did not realize for several days what had happened. It just seemed like the right thing at the right time to assist me in prayer. At the same time, Marineview was growing in numbers and in its understanding of renewal.

In the spring of 1977, I was praying for an opportunity to travel to Kansas City to attend the huge charismatic conference on the Holy Spirit. I knew that this would be a big conference; over forty thousand were to attend, and I wanted to be part of it. I pleaded with the Lord to let me go, but nothing seemed to avail. Finally, he spoke very specifically and said, "Not now, but later!" I wrote these words in my diary and tried to figure out what they meant. My limited conclusion at that time was that God was going to bring another wave of the Spirit and then I would get to participate.

Those Controversial Gifts

Still not in the mainstream of the charismatic movement, we continued to practice and teach what God had been doing in our own lives. On Christmas morning 1981, I was awakened about 4:00 AM. I knew at that moment I was to write a book for evangelicals like myself who did not believe in the present gifting of the Holy Spirit. God impressed on my heart that large numbers of evangelicals were going to be awakened by the Spirit and begin to exercise the gifts of the Spirit. This leading was so strong that I was given by the Spirit full chapter titles, outlines, and even specific dictations of particular paragraphs. Within a few days the project had begun.

In the spring of 1983, *Those Controversial Gifts* was published by Inter-Varsity Press. Two weeks later I was stricken with a mysterious illness that caused me to be bedridden for three months and took another year to fully recover from. I now know that a major spiritual attack was launched against us at that time as the devil resisted the notion of evangelicals being released in the Spirit.

"You're Too Cerebral!"

In July of 1983, I joined the pastoral team of Burnaby Christian Fellowship. That same summer the World Council of Churches (WCC) held its Sixth Assembly in Vancouver. During the assembly, a number of churches in Vancouver sponsored three evenings of special speakers giving our response to the WCC agenda. John Wimber was one of three invited guests.

I had never met John before, but David Watson had once raved about him and the church he pastored in Anaheim. I met him in his hotel for dinner and since I was still suffering from my sickness, John invited me up to his room to receive prayer. "I sense you have a spirit of rejection. Has anyone ever shown major rejection toward you?" was his opening question. I mumbled some comment and John continued to pray. Over the next two years the truthfulness of John's discernment became apparent. On two separate occasions, unknown to anyone but Bonnie and me, God graphically and quickly, within about thirty minutes, healed me of a childhood rejection experience. The effects have been dramatic and have freed me for pastoral ministry I have never known before.

The day following John's prayer I picked him up at the hotel for the evening meeting. After driving for a few minutes John said, "You know, George, your problem is you're too cerebral!" These words came like a shot to my pride. Had I not made the arduous trek out of cessationism? Had I not written correction to my peers on the subject? And had I not endured enough spiritual warfare because of my convictions? To add insult to injury, later that night John had all the pastors pray for a dozen people with deafness. This public procedure before the congregation separated the men from the boys, those who really believed in healing as opposed to those who liked to talk about it.

Even though I heard later that at least one deaf ear was opened, I was glad when John left town and vowed that I didn't want any more to do with him. One's ego could only take so much pounding.

Cancer Strikes

John was not gone more than a few weeks when doctors discovered a malignant tumor connected to Bonnie's Fallopian tube. Although they wanted to operate immediately, it was a few days before we could secure a hospital bed for her. During those days God came close to my wife and assured her of healing. Surgery removed the tumor, a rare ugly mass of which only twenty-five had been seen in the last forty years at the Vancouver Cancer Clinic. Amazingly, the doctors said they had gotten all the cancer and that just a few radiation treatments were necessary.

When we returned to the hospital two weeks later the doctors' assessment had changed dramatically. Now they were suggesting a full year of chemotherapy and radiation to ensure that the cancer would not return. We traveled to the Princess Margaret Hospital in Toronto, one of the finest cancer clinics in North America, to get a second opinion. The Director of the Ontario Cancer Institute supervised the case and concluded that the danger of the return of cancer was far more serious than the Vancouver doctors had suggested.

With this hard news churning in our stomachs, we took a ride to Niagara Falls. For a good part of the day we stood before the rushing falls, the spray in our faces indistinguishable from our tears. That night we returned to a medical friend's home and hammered out our options. As the conversation went back and forth, I could tell that my wife was growing in faith and that she was about to enter this journey without any medical help whatsoever. And by God's mercy she has continued in excellent health for the last three and a half years.

Signs and Wonders and Church Growth

It was only concern for Bonnie's continued health that led me to consider attending John Wimber's 1984 "Signs and Wonders and Church Growth" course at the Anaheim Vineyard Christian Fellowship. I cannot describe the agony I endured during that week. In many ways it was like being born again *again*. Repentance, faith, and the struggle to believe replayed themselves before me like an old dream. Even though I agreed with the idea of the present working of the Spirit, God was working on my "cerebralism" and I was forced to conclude again that God was interested in "showing up." Naturally this is very dangerous, because a God who could heal a paralyzed woman before my eyes could also point out my sin.

God spoke very clearly to me midway through the conference. "You can go to the meeting tonight and I will reveal your sin publicly in a matter of minutes, or you can stay in your motel room and I will do the same thing, only it will take half the night and cause you much agony." Preservation of a good face won out and I battled most of the evening with the entanglements that had gained a foothold in my life.

Vowing that I would go public with my repentance, I was ready for the prophecy the next morning that called pastors to repent. The cleansing I experienced that morning, along with hundreds of others, was as dramatic as anything I had ever known. Subsequent weeks of ministry proved this not to be a passing "high," but a genuine work of God's grace.

The benefits of this one conference have been multiple. I feel a hatred for any personal sin and a resistance to ever being enslaved again. I have begun to pray for more people than I would have ever imagined. Shortly after returning to Vancouver and in the midst of teaching a course at Regent College, I saw a woman instantly healed of a curvature of the spine. I also began to see demonized people set free, and a rekindled desire for evangelism has returned.

There have been results too. When we returned from the conference two things happened. First, we experienced a God-given season of repentance as a church that lasted for eight weeks. This intense period freed many from long-standing patterns of sin. Next, we began to teach and pray for the sick and demonized. Although Burnaby Christian Fellowship was known as being "charismatic," in reality there was still much skepticism about the work of the Holy Spirit. This made some uneasy and eventually a number of members as well as staff left the church to form a new congregation. This has been a painful experience, but neither side has placed blame on the other and thus a degree of harmony still exists.

Surf's Up

Is there a Third Wave of the Holy Spirit washing up on the shores of North America? I think the answer is yes! And who is the Holy Spirit appealing to in this fresh work? I think the audience will be made up of conservative evangelicals who have for years theologically and emotionally resisted the active presence and power of the Holy Spirit. Most conservative evangelicals could not go along with the charismatic renewal of the 1960s and 1970s because they could not adopt a "second blessing–initial evidence" theology of many Pentecostals. By "second blessing" the Pentecostals mean we receive the Holy Spirit subsequent to conversion, and by "initial evidence" they mean speaking in tongues.

The theology and practice of the Third Wave suits well this group of people. It is exegetically acceptable, theologically harmonious, and culturally sensitive. But at the same time each person will be confronted with a God who actually "shows up" when they minister in his name.

Over the past few years I have seen dozens of evangelical pastors of all stripes and traditions caught up in this wave. Many of them are in turmoil as they relearn their walk with the Holy Spirit and try to bring these fruits into their church life in a peaceful way. Some have lost their jobs because the resistance was too strong. Soon these denominations will see how short-sighted they have been in removing such men and women of the gospel.

However, this move of the Holy Spirit is sovereign and more and more young leaders will be caught up in it. God willing, by the turn of the century the entire evangelical church in North America may be renewed by this wave and begin to practice all the gifts of the Holy Spirit.

8

Being Right Isn't Enough

Jack Deere

Jack Deere is on the pastoral staff of Grace Vineyard of Arlington, Texas. He recently left Dallas Theological Seminary, Dallas, Texas, after 11 years as associate professor of Old Testament. He and his wife, Leesa, have three children.

We had just come out of the intensive care unit on the second floor of a local hospital. We were a dejected group of seven—three pastors, three elders, and my wife. For two days we had been part of a large group praying for a member of our church who had suffered a massive aneurysm. His EEG had been flat for forty-eight hours, and the neurologist was about to pronounce him dead. The physician had agreed to let the seven of us go in and lay hands on our friend when they turned off the respirator and let us ask God to bring him back to life. They unhooked the respirator, he stopped breathing, and for the next three minutes we asked the Lord to restore his life. Nothing happened. They started the respirator again to keep his organs alive because his wife had allowed them to be donated for transplants.

Now I was sitting in a small room with the dead man's wife, telling her that her husband was with the Lord. Then I fell into silence while others consoled her. All the usual questions and emotions flooded my mind. I had been in this position before, but never quite like this. This time I had actually expected God to raise up this thirty-eight-year-old husband and father of two young girls. I had asked in faith and God had said no to this request. A double grief had settled over me in that small room. I felt the pain of that family's loss and also the sadness of a child whose father had just denied him an important and perfectly reasonable request.

It was then that I began to reflect on how much my life had changed in the last thirteen months. A year ago I could not have prayed with faith for God to raise someone from the dead; my prayer would have only been a symbolic gesture. But all that has changed radically. In the last year I have prayed for and seen God do the following: instantly heal an aneurysm, instantly heal a severe ten-year affliction of migraine headaches, instantly heal marijuana and cocaine addiction, deliver people of demons, heal the emotional scars of severe incestual sexual abuse victims, and on and on. As a result of these experiences and a fresh study of Scriptures I now not only believe that God *can* heal, but also that very frequently he *wants* to heal. So now I pray for people with much greater expectation than I used to. I attribute this change in me to the ministry of the Holy Spirit in my life. The following is a brief sketch of my spiritual pilgrimage.

Dallas Theological Seminary

I became a Christian in the middle of my junior year in high school. I was seventeen years old and had no prior religious background. Immediately I had an overwhelming desire to lead my friends to Christ and a zeal to know Christ through the Scriptures. One by one I lost most of my friends, but God gave me new friends. I read the New Testament from cover to cover several times and then started on the Old Testament. I became actively involved in a local Baptist church and in the ministry of Young Life.

By the time I graduated from college I was leading a large Young Life Club and seeing high-school kids and parents come to Christ on a regular basis. It was then that I decided to go to seminary and receive training for a vocational ministry.

For four years I concentrated on Greek and Hebrew studies, and when I finished the masters program I began doctoral work in Old Testament and Semitic studies. For the past eleven years I have taught Hebrew and the Old Testament at Dallas Theological Seminary.

Seven years ago I helped to start a nondenominational church that has grown in attendance from sixty to five hundred people. I have offered this short autobiography to say this: viewed from the outside my life was successful and orderly, but on the inside I had withered.

Spiritual Dryness

I had gone for years without personally leading anyone to Christ. After I had been in seminary for a couple of years, I found myself more attracted to study and less attracted to building relationships. I stopped looking for ways to spend time with non-Christians. I justified this withdrawal from non-Christians by convincing myself that my basic contribution to the church was not an evangelistic but a nurturing ministry—by nurturing ministry I meant a teaching ministry. The more I came to conceive of my ministry in terms of teaching the content of the Bible, the more I began to study and withdraw from all but a select group of people.

Finally I lost even the desire to nurture and was left only with the desire to study. I was giving lectures in the seminary and sermons in the church, but I was not, in Ezekiel's words, "strengthening the weak, healing the sick, binding up the injured, bringing back the strays, or searching for the lost" (34:4). For example, during the first six years of our church existence I had, as a pastor, only prayed for and laid hands on two people, even though God had commanded this as a normative practice for the church (James 5:14–16).

The dominant desire in my Christian experience was now "to be right." Jesus said the most important commandment is to "Love the Lord your God with all your heart and with all your soul and with all your mind and with all your strength. The second is this: Love your neighbor as yourself" (Mark 12:30–31). But for me the greatest commandment had become "Be right," and the second greatest was "Convince your neighbor that you are right."

It is a remarkable fact that people can spend the bulk of their time studying and memorizing the Bible and yet lose their intimacy with its Author. Yet this is exactly where my quest for absolute doctrinal purity led me. In actual practice, it was more important for me to be right than to know God. Of course, I would never have admitted this at the time. I had given a number of lectures and sermons on the difference between knowing the Bible and knowing God. The danger of falsely equating knowledge with spiritual maturity was a regular theme in my repertoire of exhortations. What I am confessing now all came to me in the hindsight clarity of repentance.

Germany

The steps that eventually led to the beginning of my repentance began on a sabbatical study leave when I took my family to Germany for the academic year 1984–1985. Being placed in a completely different culture and relieved of my usual academic and ministry responsibilities gave my wife, Leesa, and me the opportunity to ask ourselves some hard questions about the direction of our lives. Neither one of us was sure that we wanted to stay in a vocational ministry. We had lost our intimacy with Christ. We still had spiritual gifts and ministries waiting back in America for us, but we had surrendered the friendship with God without which the exercise of the gifts and ministry can only lead to drudgery and cynicism. But then two things happened to change us.

The first and most important step was that the Holy Spirit began to speak to Leesa while we were in Germany. She did not know at that time that it was the Holy Spirit speaking to her. All she knew was that she was feeling a gentle but firm conviction of her sin and at the same time a hunger for God growing within her. In the afternoons she began taking two- and three-hour walks in the Black Forest. She spent almost the whole time in prayer repenting of her spiritual lukewarmness and then asking God to give me a new heart. During this time she did not talk much about the growing hunger for God she was experiencing, nor did she criticize me for my lack of spiritual hunger. But God was changing her. He was also beginning to answer her prayers for me.

The second thing that God used to change me was two trips behind the Iron Curtain, where I delivered lectures and sermons to Christians living under Communism. The Christians I met there were the most joyful group of people that I had encountered during my year in Europe (and I had met Christians all over Europe that year; I was in ten countries). They had far less religious freedom, food, money, entertainment, goods, and opportunities for advancement than Christians in the West. Yet they were genuinely loving, hospitable, and happy.

I was surprised that they could have what seemed to me to be so few freedoms and so little material substance yet at the same time possess such a genuine delight in the grace of Christ. I knew in my heart that if I had to live under those same conditions I would not be able to rejoice in Christ as they did. Then I began to get the first glimpses of how far from the Spirit of Christ I had fallen.

Home Again

When we came back to America at the beginning of the school year in 1985 I wanted to recover that original love of God that I had lost, but I did not know how to go about it. My wife continued spending a great deal of time in prayer, giving more and more of herself to God. While I could observe this, I couldn't follow her example; I knew that there were large areas of my life that I was afraid to give to God.

But then in the spring of 1986 God met me in a special way. We had invited John White, an internationally known psychiatrist, author, and speaker, to lead a Bible conference in our church. (At that time I was part-time pastor of a nondenominational Bible church.) On Saturday afternoon he spoke about the need for all Christians to pray for one another and expect God to heal our physical, emotional, and spiritual wounds (James 5:16).

At the conclusion of the message he invited anyone who wanted prayer for any need to come down to the front of the church. There was no hymn or emotional appeal—just a simple invitation. The response was overwhelming. (We had never had any kind of invitation in our church before, nor had we prayed for anyone at the conclusion of the service.) About seventy people came to the front of the sanctuary. Some wanted prayer for physical afflictions, but most wanted prayer for emotional and spiritual pain. There was a lot of weeping and even some screaming. This display of raw emotion frightened some of the bystanders and disgusted others. But it demonstrated to me how much pain in our fellowship lay hidden beneath the surface and how we had refused one another permission to express that pain. I did not know it at the time, but the Holy Spirit had fallen on our meeting and released our people from the self-control that they relied on to keep that pain hidden deep within.

In the next few minutes he came to me also, but it is only in retrospect that now I know that it was the Holy Spirit who was speaking to me. It happened as I knelt with John White to pray over a woman. Just as I was wishing that I could learn to pray as John a gentle voice within me said, "You are using deception and manipulation to get your way and you are only playing church." I have come to recognize that voice much more quickly since then. It was the Holy Spirit convicting me of my sin. I was faced with a decision to either acknowledge or deny this message. All I said was, "Yes, I agree." My life has not been the same since.

So much hurt in our church had been unmasked during the conference that John White stayed four days longer to counsel and pray for our people. My wife and I took every opportunity available to pray over people with John. When he left we "hung out our shingle" and let it be known that we wanted to pray for people. We asked God to give us a ministry of prayer. We read books on prayer, listened to tapes on prayer and, most importantly, we started praying for as many people as possible.

Enter John Wimber

Two weeks after our conference, John Wimber came to our city to conduct a conference at a Southern Baptist church. This was our first exposure to "signs and Wimbers," as one writer has recently put it. We went with some apprehension, not knowing what to expect. What we experienced was moving worship, a biblical message on the kingdom of God, and for the first time we saw people we knew healed instantly of various physical afflictions.

John Wimber broke my stereotype of the "faith healer." Although I had never known or seen any faith healers (except in the movies) or even known anyone who had been to a healer, I had a stereotype of them in my mind. I assumed that they were all dishonest (they faked healings), ineffective (no one ever got healed), motivated by greed, biblically ignorant, emotionally unbalanced, and arrogant (claiming that *they* had the power to heal).

John was none of these things. He made it clear that it was the Lord who healed, and that *all* Christians could learn to pray effectively for the sick. He refused to allow himself to be treated as "the healer." Instead he used ministry teams to pray for those who came forward and gave practical instruction to others who wanted to pray for people.

What impressed me most about the conference was not the healings but the mercy and compassion of Christ that permeated every phase of the ministry. People were encouraged to pray not only on the basis of the power of the Holy Spirit to heal but also because of the mercy and compassion of God toward his children. And they were being taught how to pray for one another in an atmosphere of mercy and compassion. This kind of environment provided Christians the freedom to risk embarrassment and failure both in praying for one another and in being prayed for.

The lesson I learned from this was that without the freedom to make mistakes, there is no risk taking, and without risk taking there is no growth. Years ago on the ski slopes of Colorado I learned how important it was to risk falling and looking silly if I were going to learn to ski well. An accomplished instructor helped me get back on my feet one morning after a particularly disheartening fall. He said, "Don't be discouraged, the only good skier you'll ever see is a bad one who didn't give up." It shouldn't have taken so long for me to see this truth on a spiritual plane.

The only good evangelist you'll ever see is a bad one who didn't give up. The only good pray-er you'll ever see is a bad one who didn't give up. This is true of all the individual gifts and ministries of the Holy Spirit. But an atmosphere of mercy and compassion—not judgmental criticism—is required for ineffective servants to take risks to become effective servants.

This was a major revelation for one whose chief value was to be right and who usually felt the need to control situations. I knew that I had to give up my comfortable life-style and to take risks for God again if I were ever going to hear the Holy Spirit speak to me on a regular basis. It was sobering to realize that I had not been willing to risk anything for Jesus. I avoided situations where I had to have the power of the Holy Spirit or had to hear the Spirit speak to me. I was giving lectures and sermons, to be sure, but I had been doing that for years without conscious reliance on the Holy Spirit. Now I wanted to minister in the power of the Holy Spirit.

I was tired of living a life without feeling the presence of Christ and of having a ministry without the power of the Holy Spirit. Year after year I had watched members in my church who faithfully listened to my sermons and Bible lectures live their lives with very little significant change. The depressed stayed depressed, the absentee-workaholic fathers continued to neglect their families, the sick almost never got healed unless it was through medicine, various lusts and addictions continued to control too many of the people, we rarely led anyone to Christ, and we never saw significant improvement among the neurotic people apart from long-term therapy with a professional counselor.

I could no longer accept that redeemed children of the living God should have to live such insipid, powerless lives. Why did we have so little power? And how could we experience more of God? I knew the answer went beyond personal Bible study and faithful teaching of the Bible, because those were the two things I had spent most of my time doing in our church. My wife and I were determined to find what was missing.

Doubts

About a month after John Wimber had come to our city we were preparing to visit him in California to get some answers to our questions. While working in our front yard one day I was thinking about the relative ineffectiveness of our lives and ministry in light of our prospective trip to Anaheim. (By now I had heard a good deal more about the ministry of the Vineyard. Most of the news was positive, but some was controversial.) I began wondering about what would happen if my initial impressions of John Wimber and his ministry were wrong. What if the healings I thought I had witnessed were not real? What if the stories I had heard about other healings, unusually successful evangelistic efforts, casting out demons, supernatural guidance, and others, were all exaggerations? Or, worse, what if they were big hoaxes? What if the mercy and compassion I thought I experienced in the conference setting a month earlier had been merely an emotional experience and not a true work of the Holy Spirit? Or, to imagine the worst scenario, what if by opening myself to the supernatural I was being duped by a demon!

I stopped my yard work and said to God, "If all this is not real, if you're not healing, empowering, genuinely changing, and speaking to your children in a much more striking way than I've experienced in the last twelve years, then I'm getting out. I'm leaving the ministry. There's too much criticism and too little love, too much to change and too little power to change it. I'm going to accept an offer to go into business."

As soon as I said this I realized that this was not how I truly felt. "Lord," I prayed, "if all this is not true, then I don't want a business career. What I really want is to go home, just take me to heaven. If you are not going to give me a ministry characterized by your presence, power, and love in a manner similar to what the Holy Spirit produced in the early church, then I don't want to live here any longer. Take me home." As I stood there in my front yard that afternoon, the Holy Spirit had just wooed me back to Christ without my even knowing it.

California Bound

The trip to Anaheim was not disappointing. We were able to interview at random people who had been dramatically healed. We participated in worship services and prayed for people afterward with members of the ministry teams. We asked the associate pastors many questions. Also, we were able to talk at length with John and Carol Wimber. We were as deeply impressed by their humility, love, and honesty as we were enlightened by their answers to our questions.

When we left the Vineyard we were convinced that God wanted to give us much more of himself than we had ever known. Perhaps the reason for our lack was as simple as James 4:2: "You do not have, because you do not ask God." Now we were encouraged to ask and believe God for more than we had ever imagined possible in the past.

It has been exactly one year since that trip to the Vineyard. Perhaps I can best summarize the transformation the Holy Spirit has brought in my life this past year with this incident. I was having lunch recently with a group of my colleagues when one of them quoted the now popular declaration that "if the Holy Spirit were taken out of the world today, 98 percent of all Christian activity would continue without any appreciable difference." Everyone around the table acknowledged the lamentable truth of this assertion.

That afternoon I asked myself what I was doing that required the power of the Holy Spirit for success. Or, to put it another way, what was there in my life that could only be explained in terms of the work of the Holy Spirit, so that if he were taken out of my life there would be an immediate difference? I came up with at least six things, none of which were part of my life a year ago.

Healing the Sick

The first and most obvious work of the Holy Spirit in my life relates to a *healing ministry*. Currently I am praying almost every day for people's physical, emotional, or spiritual problems. As often as possible I pray for people with a ministry team made up of individuals who have hearts for the healing ministry and who have shown themselves to be effective in prayer and listening to God. Not everyone we pray for gets healed, but we have seen the Holy Spirit perform some dramatic healings. Also, we are seeing healing increase among us as prayer for the sick becomes a way of life. If the Holy Spirit were taken out of the world our healing prayers would go unanswered, and I would stop praying for the sick.

Perhaps I might mention three of the major excuses I used for not praying for the sick before. They were: God is not healing today, the spiritual aspects of one's life are more important than the physical, and the disappointment of those who get prayed for but are not healed may damage faith and produce bitterness in them. In my case these obstacles were not overcome by discussion or theological argument, but rather through actual experience of praying for people.

One could debate the scriptural evidence endlessly as to whether or not God is healing today, but when I started praying for the sick I *saw* God heal. I never saw God heal before because I didn't pray for the sick. I never put myself in a place where he was healing. I did not have any credible witnesses to the Holy Spirit's contemporary healing ministry because by definition I knew that he was not healing, and I wouldn't believe anyone who claimed differently. But when I decided to obey God's command to pray for the sick (James 5:14–16) and to make healing prayer a way of life, Christ showed himself to me in his healing power.

My second excuse—that the spiritual is more important than the physical—is, of course, true as a theological statement, but illogical as a reason for not praying for the relief of suffering. When I was ill I sought relief through rest, medicine, or a physician's care. Even when ill, I believed my spiritual condition to be more important than my physical, yet I still sought healing through medical means. Why should I have ever thought it was inconsistent to ask God's help in addition to medical means?

Experience has also proved my third excuse to be unfounded. To my knowledge, no one's faith has been damaged when we prayed for them and they were not healed. On the contrary, even people who have not been healed feel loved and significant before us and before God. And those feelings of love and significance grow as we commit ourselves to pray for them repeatedly until God gives us a definite yes or no.

Evangelism

A second activity that would stop if the Holy Spirit were taken out of my life is *evangelism*. I had gone for several years without leading anyone to Christ. After I began feeling the conviction and presence of the Holy Spirit again, I started leading individuals to Christ again, sometimes in response to specific direction from the Holy Spirit.

What I have learned from these recent experiences is that the gift of evangelism is not so much the ability to persuade as it is a special sensitivity to the leading of the Holy Spirit, so that the Holy Spirit can direct his messenger to those people with whom he is already at work. In Scripture we see this in the Spirit's leading of Philip to the Ethiopian eunuch, which resulted in his conversion (Acts 8:29). Another example is the specific directions given to Peter in Acts 10:19, which led to the beginning of a group at Cornelius' home. In Acts 16:6–10, Paul was guided supernaturally by the Holy Spirit to found the church in Philippi.

Deliverance

A third area in which I find myself completely dependent on the ministry of the Holy Spirit is in *delivering demonized people*. When our church began going through a period of revival, one of the first things that happened was the Holy Spirit revealed the presence of demonic activity within the individuals in our fellowship. I have been involved in eight to ten cases of healing demonized persons, and I know from firsthand experience that without the power of the Holy Spirit we would have had no success, for, as Jesus demonstrated, this area of ministry is to be specifically attributed to the work of the Holy Spirit (Matt. 12:28).

Guidance

A fourth ministry of the Holy Spirit that has become important to me is *guidance*. The chief means of guidance is, of course, the Bible (2 Tim. 3:16-17), but the Spirit also speaks directly to us (Acts 8:29; 10:2, 19; 16:6-10; James 1:5).

A recent example of this for me occurred in a joint meeting of the pastors, elders, and deacons at our church. The meeting was a little tense, and I felt the tension was due to the failure of several of the deacons to recognize the authority of the elders in the matter under discussion. As a pastor, I wanted to resolve the tension by reading to the deacons 1 Timothy 5:17, which says that it is "the elders who direct the affairs of the church." But the Holy Spirit clearly said, "No." I started to read the text to the group anyway, but again the impressions of "no" and "trust me" came into my mind. I closed the Bible and waited. Within two minutes one of the deacons spoke up and said, "You know, this whole issue ought to be resolved by 1 Timothy 5:17." Then he read the passage to the group. The fact that a deacon brought this text to everyone had a much greater impact than if I had done so.

Insight

A fifth activity in my life that would be missing without the Holy Spirit is the *special insights or impressions that God gives me for ministry.* Perhaps this can be classified as a specific form of guidance. However, these impressions often come into my mind uninvited, almost as intrusions that first seem completely irrelevant to the situation at hand but when acted on result in ministry to someone.

For example, recently a young Christian man came into my office quite by accident, and in the midst of a superficial conversation that had nothing to do with the man's spiritual condition a very serious sin flashed into my mind. I saw the name of the sin printed in large, slightly tilted block letters. It was a fleeting impression that at first I dismissed. Then it returned about five minutes later, and did so regularly for the next twenty minutes. Finally, I interrupted the young man and asked if he were struggling with anything. "No," he replied, mildly offended by my inquiry.

But the impression wouldn't go away. I asked again, "Is there any guilt in your life?" Again he denied it. Finally I blurted out, "Are you into [name of the sin]?" The minute I asked the question I knew that he was committing the sin and that he intended to lie to me for the third time. Before he could answer, I said, "I think if you'll confess this sin, God will deliver you of it today." This gave him the encouragement he needed to admit his sin in my presence. As it turned out, the sin that I had "seen" in block letters in my mind was only the tip of the iceberg. My young friend was in bondage to evil, but as we prayed the power of the Holy Spirit came on him, breaking his bondage to evil. Since I have begun to have fellowship with the Holy Spirit (2 Cor. 13:14), this kind of experience has not been an uncommon occurrence for me.

Worship

Lastly, the ministry of the Holy Spirit in the area of *worship* has become important to me. Until recently our Sunday morning worship service was actually a teaching service that left very little room for worship. Now we are beginning to learn what the Psalmist meant when he exhorted God's people to "worship the Lord with gladness; come before him with joyful songs . . . enter his gates with thanksgiving and his courts with praise; give thanks to him and praise his name" (Ps. 100:2, 4). We are beginning to come to worship to give something to God rather than get something. We are beginning to sense the presence of the Holy Spirit during worship both in our Sunday morning service and in our small home meetings during the week.

With the exception of evangelism, these six areas are new experiences of the Holy Spirit's power in my life and ministry. The fact that I had previously settled for so much less is a testimony to the unbelief and spiritual poverty of my Christian experience. Pauline Christianity affirms that "the kingdom of God is not a matter of talk but of power" (1 Cor. 4:20). From the book of Acts as well as his Letters, it is clear that Paul counted on the power of the Holy Spirit to love, heal, evangelize, cast out demons, worship, provide detailed directions for ministry, and more. I hope I will never again expect any less from him.

9

Exorcising the Ghost of Newton

Don Williams

Don Williams served as senior pastor of Mt. Soledad Presbyterian Church, La Jolla, California, for the past seven years. Currently he is pursuing a radio, writing, and speaking ministry. He holds a Ph.D from Columbia University, specializing in the New Testament, and has written seven books. He and his wife, Kathryn, live in La Jolla.

Born in 1937, I was raised in the stable middle-class world of Protestant liberalism. My parents were highly moral, idealistic, and pragmatic. My father gave me his Newtonian worldview. He taught me, "A place for everything and everything in its place." The major issues between us were leaving the newspaper and my shoes on the living room floor, denting the doors by hooking clothes hangers over them, and slicing off the wrong end of the butter.

While my dad was busy organizing reality and finding the right place for things, which, of course, assumes that a reasonable, ordered world would reward his efforts, my mother was a social Darwinist. She taught me, "Leave the world a little better than you found it." This dictum propelled her into civic activities such as serving on the local school board and leading a Girl Scout troop. She certainly expected me to follow her example. This created a certain tension for me. There is an uneasy truce between ordering the world and improving the world at the same time, but I tried by best. What is important to note here is that I was raised with the modern myths of white middle-class, twentieth-century America. My education, the media, and my social relationships all tended to reinforce these unchallenged assumptions about reality. I bought that part of the American dream determined by progress, service to society, and the discovery of its underlying rational order. Like my father, it was important for me to be in control and to maintain control. My arena was not the athletic field or the marketplace; my arena was the life of the mind. Here reason was king and I could control people and situations through my intellect. In debate and dialectic I asserted my manhood by outthinking and outarguing my opponents.

At fifteen years of age, through the ministry of Young Life (an evangelical outreach to high-school students) I was converted to Christ. For me this was God's dramatic intervention in my life. I was first attracted to some caring Christians on my high-school campus who were the leaders I wanted to become. They talked about Jesus as if he were their contemporary. Heretofore, I thought him to be a figure locked into history. For these friends, however, he was alive and present. This intrigued me. Then at a weekend camp where Jim Rayburn, the founder of Young Life and a dynamic evangelist, preached, Christ came into my life. This was a watershed moment for me. The problem, however, was that in terms of my Newtonian-Darwinian worldview I experienced only an "evangelical interruption." While I now had a relationship with Christ, began to read the Bible, have fellowship with other Christians, and share my faith, I still had a decisive need to be in control and approached the world and my faith in a highly rationalistic way. Thus as Francis Schaffer warned, I was in danger of kicking Christ into the "upper story" of my intellect and my devotional life, while I continued to live on the "lower story" ordering and improving my world with my power and in my way.

Princeton University

As I advanced in my higher education with a scholarship to Princeton University, these basic themes of my life were only reinforced. I ordered my world through an increasingly well-trained intellect and I improved my world through Christian compassion. But again, it was *my* world and I was in control. I asked God to bless my plans rather than to give me his, and since by now I felt certain that I was called into the professional ministry, I assumed that I must be doing his will.

The move from Princeton University to Princeton Theological Seminary was easy and predictable. Not only are the two campuses separated by merely one block, their operative worldviews are just as proximate. I identified with the evangelical element at the seminary in terms of my theological tradition and, at the same time, found my Newtonian controls enhanced by receiving the proper tools to manage the professional ministry.

In my "enlightenment" theological education I was trained to control everything. Paul's dictum to do all things "decently and in order" is lived out by us Presbyterians to a fault. Thus I was given exegetical tools with which to manage the Bible, theological tools with which to manage the faith, homiletical tools with which to manage my sermons, psychological and sociological tools with which to manage people, and business tools with which to manage the church. Today's seminary curriculum is far advanced in this application of the scientific method to the professional clergy. Thus today we have courses in time management, conflict management, and financial management for local pastors who operate their franchises for the larger denominations.

Again, my worldview, my operative comprehension of reality, was never challenged by all of this. The church lay before me and I was equipped to move into it and take control of its life. After exercising my Ph.D. option at Union Seminary and Columbia University for another two years, I began my professional ministry, inheriting the college work of Dr. Henrietta C. Mears at Hollywood Presbyterian Church in California.

Hollywood

The first several years with college students were highly successful for me. I had scores of sorority and fraternity types coming to the church from UCLA and USC and the staff and elders of the church were delighted with an average Sunday attendance of over two hundred students in my class. This was now the early 1960s of Kennedy's Camelot. Dark clouds, however, were on the horizon.

As the Vietnam war heated up and the nation divided, I was caught between a powerful, prominent, established church, on the one hand, and the streets of Hollywood which were becoming littered with counterculture dropouts, on the other. A friend introduced me to the music of Bob Dylan and forced me to listen to the lyrics behind his nasal twang. Suddenly I began to hear the cries of a new generation. Then I met my first "hippie," a throwaway girl who was pregnant and on the streets. As she came to Christ we became friends and I saw a bizarre, uncontrolled world of "peace-love, brother" at my doorstep.

Folk music, rock music, the drug culture, protest marches, student riots, sexual brokenness, emotional disorders, draft card burners, communes, hippie "tribes"—all invaded my safe, controlled world and ministry. Here was the first frontal assault on my Newtonian perception of reality. What about reason and its role? Ex–Harvard professor Timothy Leary dismissed it lightly: "Reason is a tissue-thin artifact easily destroyed by a slight alteration in the body's biochemistry." As the psychedelic culture swirled around me and the Woodstock generation took form, I began to see what he meant.

Later, I was to realize that what I experienced in the sixties trying to minister to the streets of Hollywood through a coffee house, crash-pads, and the communal living of the "Jesus movement" had been in process for a long time. Carl Becker in his Yale lectures of 1932 noted that, "It has taken eight centuries to replace the conception of existence as divinely composed and purposeful drama by the conception of existence as a blindly running flux of disintegrating energy, but there are signs that the substitution is now fully accomplished; and if we wished to reduce eight centuries of intellectual history to an epigram, we could not do better than to borrow the words of Aristophanes, 'Whirl is king, having deposed Zeus.'" Moreover, Becker asks, "What is man that the electron should be mindful of him? Man is but a foundling in the cosmos, abandoned by the forces that created him. Unparented, unassisted and undirected by omniscient or benevolent authority, he must fend for himself, and with the aid of his own limited intelligence find his way about in an indifferent universe" (*The Heavenly City of the Eighteenth-Century Philosophers*, p. 15). Indeed, on the streets of Hollywood, I found that "Whirl is king" and my Newtonian worldview was beginning to crack.

This became very personal to me at one point when we were reaching the "counterculture" through a coffee house called "The Salt Company." There I became involved in helping a young man who was suicidal. Several nights of strain left me with a physical reaction; my heart began to miss every third beat. Better sleep habits didn't help. I came so close to an emotional breakdown that I finally went to see a doctor (who was a cross between Amos and Jeremiah). He ordered me out of town for a complete rest. Two weeks in Paris watching my friend Stan Smith play professional tennis reversed the symptoms, but I was learning that I was not in control and that since there was not a place for everything I could not possibly get everything into its place. At last I was encountering the irrational in the depths of my own emotions and sanity. I battled burnout to a standstill but I didn't win the war.

Claremont MacKenna College

The sixties passed, the Vietnam wound healed, and life became manageable again. After marrying Kathryn Rimmer in 1972, I left the church and took up teaching religion at Claremont MacKenna College (then Claremont Men's College). My classes were successful, my lectures popular, and the quiet conservative campus was a comfortable environment for the life of the mind. Here was what I was used to in the 1950s, and after weathering controversy over my being an evangelical teacher on a secular campus, I settled in well. Once again reason reigned and the Newton in me was resurrected.

At this point, however, a student in English at Claremont Graduate School slipped around my defenses. It began innocuously enough. He was the last of the hippies in the mid-seventies with a long beard, sleeping bag, and sandals. Coming from Washington state, he had become a "Jesus freak" out of severe drug use in the sixties. Steve was drawn to me because of my evangelical stand. As we talked, I found much in common with him from my Hollywood days. There was one point, however, where he bothered me a little. It was when he noted that there was something missing in my life and added, "Don, you need the power of the Holy Spirit."

Well, I had heard this long before from a charismatic clique at Hollywood. They had been determined to get me "baptized in the Holy Spirit" by taking me to meetings where people prayed in tongues and did other weird things. These people, loving though they were, impressed me as the arty, emotional fringe of the church and I quickly escaped their designs. Moreover, I was theologically well defended against all of this since I had known Dale Bruner personally from our Princeton days and had studied carefully his *A Theology of the Holy Spirit*. To my satisfaction his work demolished the "second blessing" theology of Pentecostalism and the later charismatic movement sparked by Dennis Bennett. In sum, then, I tolerated my friend's jibes about needing the power of the Spirit and went on about my business.

One night, however, Steve had dinner at our house with my wife and me. When she left us alone, he asked if he could read some passages from Acts. I surrendered to his request because of our friendship, knowing full well what the selections would be. I was not disappointed. First there was the promise of the Holy Spirit from chapter 1. Next the day of Pentecost was narrated in chapter 2. Then there was the coming of the Spirit to Samaria through the apostles laying on of hands in chapter 8. The account of the "Gentile Pentecost" followed in chapter 10 and the readings concluded with Paul's bringing the Spirit to the Ephesian disciples in chapter 19. The themes of power, verification by prophecy and tongues, and the resulting evangelistic explosion were all dutifully noted. I half listened, bid Steve "good night," and then retired.

The Spirit Comes

The next morning, Kathryn was out of the house early and I went to my study for a regular devotional time. As I opened my Bible, however, I felt strange. A burning sensation began to grow in my extremities and my pulse sped up. I felt anxious and a bit light-headed. Was it the spaghetti sauce? I struggled as the impulses grew. My mind then drifted to my conversation with Steve. Could God be doing something more to me? Was there a power I did not know? This period of my life was a quiet one. The old wars were over. I was in no perceivable emotional or spiritual crisis and yet here I was with this happening to me. I knew that I had a choice to make: either cut it off and walk away or go with it. In my dilemma I reasoned that if this was from God then I didn't want to miss it, and if it wasn't then no harm would be done (I didn't really think that the devil, who at that time I only half believed in, was in the picture). So I prayed, "Lord, if this is you and you want to do something more with me, go ahead." My spiritual Rubicon had now been passed. Next, my eyes drifted to an old, unopened copy of Dennis and Rita Bennett's *The Holy Spirit and You*. Some eager soul had given it to me years back. I thumbed the book and received some helpful information as my experience level continued to rise. Finally, I took my Bible and drove to an old prayer spot across town in the hills of Glendale where I grew up. Hiking up alone on the firebreak I began to pray aloud. A great desire to praise God came over me, and I did it freely. Joy then began to explode inside of me and, as Jesus promised, I felt a river of living water bubble up (John 7:38). Laughing and crying I found myself in ecstasy and the desire to worship, love, and praise God became so intense that English was no longer adequate to express my joy. At that moment, the Lord gave me the gift of an unknown tongue to continue my worship. The nonsense syllables (to me) rushed out of my mouth. It was sheer delight. At the same time, I was so relieved that I was alone and kept wondering, "What would my friends think if they could see me now?"

At this time, my Newtonian perception of reality, already cracked by the counterculture of the sixties, was now exploded by the Holy Spirit. The experience I denied and the gift I maligned were now both mine by a sovereign intervention of the Living God: direct, supernatural, and totally gracious. It fitted my Calvinism perfectly, and my old dispensationalism ("Yes, it was for the first century but not for us today"), which masked my unbelief and my accommodation to the modern scientific worldview of a closed system of cause and effect, lay in ruins. Rather than going out of control, which was a deep fear, I went under the Spirit's control and there was great joy and peace as a result.

Nothing Much

What then was I to do with this experience? The immediate answer was "Nothing much." The reason for this was clear. I was in no church or fellowship where I could use or even interpret what had happened to me. I imagined at the time that God had done this to give me a calling card to the charismatics. Since, as a Bible teacher, I had been able to cross many denominational lines, this experience would give me access to this segment of the church as well. Tongues would be my union card.

Despite my sixties circle crisis and the empowering of the Spirit, it was easy in my Claremont teaching and quiet life-style to lapse back into my Newtonian perceptions. I continued to maintain my controls and to entertain my latent skepticism toward the supernatural. A whole series of events and relationships then brought my wife and me to La Jolla, near San Diego, in 1979, where in 1980 I began to preach at Mt. Soledad Presbyterian Church.

This struggling congregation began to grow with a combination of intercessory prayer, solid Bible teaching, clear evangelistic messages, and the development of a small group Bible study/discussion structure during the week. By 1983 there were several hundred members and a much larger worshiping congregation in three services. Then my life went into crisis.

For several years my wife and I had been struggling in our marriage. With justification she held that I put my ministry and my career before her. Moreover, I tended to be emotionally withdrawn and unresponsive. I also carried some deep wounds from my younger years. In this context then we floundered and I experienced the deepest pain of my life.

Fuller Seminary

At that time, a friend of mine at Fuller Seminary had been telling me about John Wimber's "Signs and Wonders" course, which had become so popular and controversial. A central thesis of the class was that since Jesus proclaimed the kingdom of God and healed people, we are to do the same today. In this way Satan's kingdom is being destroyed and God's kingdom is advancing. Moreover, what keeps us from this is our fear of the supernatural, our latent unbelief (however masked it is theologically), and our need to maintain control (welcome, ghost of Newton!). Since the class was having such a big impact on my friend, he was anxious that I visit it and experience not only the teaching but the ministry ("laboratory") time afterward where the sick were being prayed for and many were healed. While I was unable to attend the class, I did go one Sunday night to the Vineyard Church where John pastored several thousand people.

In much emotional pain then in the spring of 1983, I sneaked into the gymnasium of Canyon High School in Anaheim Hills for an evening service. There, at 6:00 PM, I discovered two thousand people all singing praise songs for forty minutes, nonstop. They were accompanied by a worship band with John at the keyboard. While I had never heard their songs, and while no lyrics were provided, I was able to join in about 80 percent of the worship. As I looked around I saw faces full of joy and a freedom of expression without theatrics I had never known. My heart melted before the Lord in those moments.

Next, John taught. I expected a "rap" on the end of the world. Instead, I received thoughtful, sound teaching more like a Fuller Seminary classroom than a nondenominational church. Then, receiving several "words of knowledge" for praying for the sick, John led a time of ministry for healing. The worship opened me, the teaching assured me, and since I was sick, the time for healing allured me. I came back next week and introduced myself to John. He took me in and in my pain became my pastor, brother, friend, and teacher. I saw in John glimpses of the great revivalists: a boldness in

Christ and a vitality in faith leading to an uncanny sensitivity to the Holy Spirit. Moreover, John combined this with a solid theological and biblical sense, disarming humor, wise psychological and sociological observations, and a commanding presence. God's healing work now began in earnest in my life and what had happened to me in the sixties and seventies finally in the eighties made sense. A divine tapestry was being woven in the midst of my conflict between control and chaos.

Enter Francis MacNutt

At the end of that summer, Francis MacNutt, a former Dominican priest in the Catholic church, came to speak in San Diego. Through some friends I was able to invite him to hold an evening healing service at our church. On a Sunday night then he arrived and after a time of worship, Francis gave a simple message on Jesus as healer. Then he invited people to come and be prayed for. The service lasted from 6:00 to after 11:00 PM as Francis ministered to over a hundred people. I stood aside and watched, thinking, "This is just like the Gospels." In Francis I saw Jesus touching people and bringing his love and power to them once again.

Through what God had shown me in John and Francis I knew that my ministry would never be the same again. In them I saw Jesus' ministry of healing and deliverance through the power and anointing of the Holy Spirit. I saw, in John's phrase, that Jesus is the "Word Worker." In my past ministry I had known a lot of the Word but little of the Work, which for me had been focused merely in personal witnessing, teaching, and living an ethical life. But where is the power? And why do we need it anyway? In praying for the sick I found the answer. Healing is only through the power of the Holy Spirit. All ministry is Jesus' ministry and if I can give up control, again and again he will do his ministry through me. To a Newtonian church he brings kingdom power and to a generation where "Whirl is king" he brings kingdom order and peace.

Now I began the long pilgrimage of incorporating what I was

learning into my life, my marriage, and the ministry of the church. This meant receiving inner healing for myself, which came one night as a dear brother, Mark McCoy, prayed over me in emotional pain. This meant learning to pray for the sick and facing the problems of those who are not overtly healed. This meant learning to rely on the Holy Spirit and his gifts, to wait for his blessing, and to give up my presumption that I can control him. This meant giving the church back to Jesus as its effective Head. This meant the struggle to enter into a deeper prayer life of not only speaking to the Lord but listening to him as well. This meant the challenge (still in progress) of becoming an intercessor. This meant losing members who feared the supernatural or who knew that this ministry was not for them or for today. This meant facing spiritual pride, immaturity, and the emotional excesses of some of those gifted to heal. This meant fighting competition among people about their gifts much as Paul faced in Corinth. This meant more clearly defined spiritual opposition to Satan as he attacked our more open displays of the Holy Spirit's power. This meant cultural and spiritual shifts as we entered into the use of new worship music. This meant training a whole new group of lay leaders who wanted to do Jesus' ministry in our midst. This meant defending the unity of the church for those to whom all of this was new and scary. This meant honoring the Spirit's work in those who had no empowering experience to call upon and accepting them fully rather than making them feel like second-class Christians. This meant healing for our church and the church at large across denominational and theological lines. This meant a recovery of the history of revival to see that God has always been renewing his church down through the generations from John Wesley to George Whitefield to Charles Finney to D. L. Moody to those ministering today. This meant recovering the Gospels and large sections of Acts and the Letters for the ministry of the church as well as for the theology of the church. This meant also the attempt to give away to other pastors and churches what God was giving to us. This meant risks of faith in living in a more biblical worldview than my old Newtonian–social Darwinian upbringing. This meant, ultimately, getting closer to the heart of Jesus and letting my heart be broken with his upon the pain of the world.

For me, there is no going back to the safety of my old life and ministry, but I am comforted by a thought from Dietrich Bonhoeffer: to be secure in Jesus is to be radically insecure in this world. So be it!

IV

Pastoral Encounters

Pastors have the greatest calling and most difficult job in the world. They are called to care for men's and women's souls. So it isn't surprising that most of them go through at least one crisis in their lives. In many instances the crises of deepest effect happen to pastors who appear to be successful. They have large, growing congregations, and they are esteemed by their colleagues, but in their hearts they know something is wrong. That is true for the four contributors in this section. They had thriving churches, but they weren't fooled by their success. They knew there was more to the Christian life than they were experiencing and preaching. When they turned to God and asked him what it was, they were introduced to the power encounter.

10

"Give Me Back My Church"

Terry Virgo

Terry Virgo is senior pastor of Clarendon Church, Hove, England, and director of "New Frontiers," a team ministry. He has written two books, Restoration in the Church *and* Men of Destiny.

The streets of Brighton were filled with Saturday night crowds. Scores of young people were on their way to the dance halls, jazz clubs, and bars. I loved the atmosphere; I had been part of it for some years. But on this particular night in 1966 I was visiting the scene for the last time.

I had just become a committed Christian—but how the downtown night life drew me! I forced myself to drive my motorbike home. Gradually the bright lights of Brighton receded and were replaced by the quieter roads of my home area. My house seemed like a morgue in comparison with the glitter I had left behind. My parents, not yet Christians, were watching television. I left them to it and sank into a chair in another room, alone and desperate. "So this is abundant life!" I thought.

Eventually I knelt by the chair and began to pray in earnest. "Dear God, there must be more than this! I will never be able to keep up this Christian life if this is all there is to it."

I had tried church on Sunday but none of my friends had come with me. They could not believe that I had "gone religious" and taunted me that I would soon be back with them. The people at church were okay but too formal. I had never felt so lonely and despondent in all my life. But I knew beyond a doubt that I had found God. I had been born again. It was real.

Light Begins to Dawn

After I had prayed and poured my heart out for some time, I sat up and began to read the Bible. For the first time in my life I read through the book of Acts in one sitting. I was thrilled! At the end of the evening I knelt again: "O Lord, this is so exciting. Please lead me into all that you have for me. Please let me taste what they enjoyed. I simply can't keep up the Christian life without a dynamic experience that will release me from the past and plunge me into a life like the believers in the book of Acts."

Although nothing outwardly happened to me that night, I went to bed peacefully assured that God had heard me and that there was a future and hope. A year later, after more lows than highs, I had the joy of meeting a zealous young Pentecostal who led me to being baptized with the Holy Spirit, a fresh encounter with the Holy Spirit in which I experienced new spiritual life and empowering for ministry. I was filled with the Holy Spirit and joy, bubbling over not only with the gift of tongues but with a new awareness of "Abba, Father." Suddenly God was intimate, Jesus was wonderful, and I could not stop praising him!

Within a few weeks I had laid hands on several friends at my local Baptist church and many were baptized with the Holy Spirit. We began to enjoy worship in new dimensions: we were less formal and more spontaneous, meeting in small groups for hours and singing songs. Our gatherings were marked by a sense of intimacy and personalness with God; his presence permeated our beings, and he affected our life-styles away from the gatherings.

Because of this, we moved onto the streets of Brighton witnessing. It was revolutionary! All my spare time was taken up with door-to-door evangelism and, a year later, I left work to be available to God in full-time service. A close friend and I prayed together every morning and pursued door-to-door evangelism every afternoon. We expected revival to break out imminently. Sadly, it did not.

We thought all in life would be plain sailing now that we had received the Holy Spirit. That thought was shattered when, tragically, my friend's baby—after a few weeks' illness and many prayers—died. God had failed us ... or had we failed God? I was confused and heartbroken. I also recoiled from praying for the sick for quite a long time, bewildered by the death of my friend's baby.

New Wineskins

Meanwhile, there were many other lessons to learn. God began to speak to us about the new wine of his Spirit needing an appropriate new wineskin providing flexibility and freedom of movement. Our experience of the Holy Spirit stirred us to new expressions of worship. We wanted to praise the Lord unhindered by set forms of service.

After three years as a student at London Bible College (1965–1968), I joined a new Evangelical Free Church in Seaford, twenty miles east of Brighton, which was not charismatic but which invited me to become its first pastor with the full knowledge that I was charismatic and was committed to building a charismatic church. After early difficulties, the congregation gradually embraced life in the Spirit. The conventional "four-hymn service" was eventually transformed into an exciting experience of the power and presence of God. At first we made room for a ten-minute period of free worship: this gradually grew to twenty minutes and, finally, our whole worship time became spontaneous and free-flowing. The changes that took place were not all easy and painless. In our open worship we endured agonies before we enjoyed ecstasies. Eventually we arrived at times of worship that were like heaven on earth. We experienced a sense of unharried preoccupation with God, an expectation of his presence that brought all that we did alive. And we were unified; our singing, prayers, and prophecies all had a supernatural unity, an anointing that we knew could come only from God. People started to travel to be with us to enjoy the presence of God and the developing use of spiritual gifts and experiences like tongues and interpretation, prophecies, visions, and so on.

Kingdom Awareness

Throughout that period we had a growing awareness that God was doing more than simply filling individuals with the Holy Spirit and renewing our local church life. He was involved in a far greater purpose: he was restoring our vision of the kingdom of God. We became convinced that the church was no longer to be weak and irrelevant; it was to arise and shine and fulfill its destiny of representing Jesus Christ in the world. It was to be a city set on a hill that cannot be hid, a glorious bride awaiting her returning Lord. God restored our hopes that he had something wonderful for the church to fulfill in the end times, and this would involve worldwide mission. We adjusted our thinking about the church, its calling, and purpose. Soon we realized that God was saying, in words that John Wimber was later to articulate at London's Westminster Central Hall, "Give me back my church!"

Old reservations and traditions had to yield to the sovereign Lord's full right to run his church. We also had to realize that the kingdom of God was not some distant hope reserved for another age but was powerfully advancing now! We were children of the King and people of the kingdom! This prophetic purpose began to grip us and be expressed in new songs of joy and expectation. One new prophetic song swiftly replaced another as our vision developed.

Annually in the United Kingdom thousands have gathered at Bible Weeks and conferences reflecting the numerical growth of the movement. God has also been moving us onto the streets to reach our generation with the gospel. I have personally had the responsibility of leading the Downs Bible Week in southern England for the last eight years, which now gathers some ten thousand people each year.

Enter John Wimber

In the early 1980s, several South African pastors visited us at the Downs Bible Week. This resulted in my being invited to speak at one of their national Leaders' Conferences. While in Capetown I heard of the great blessing that John Wimber's team visit had been to that area.

One of the pastors strongly encouraged me to meet John Wimber, remarking that many emphases of my ministry coincided significantly with his, but that he was experiencing great success in healing the sick and leading others into that ministry. On the final night of my visit to Capetown my friend presented me with several boxes of audio cassettes of John Wimber's teaching. During the next few weeks I listened to hours of John's tapes. Three things resulted.

First, I was thrilled with the content of the teaching about divine healing in the context of the kingdom. I had often struggled to find a teaching on healing that truly satisfied me. I had read many books on healing that left me dissatisfied theologically, but John's emphasis inspired me as no one else's had.

Second, his openness about early failures and frustrations won my heart. I also had known a lot of frustration, but other healing preachers and writers seemed to provide little encouragement in that area. Their books taught how to heal the sick in ways that suggested that all was straightforward—a total contrast to my experience. At last, here was a man enjoying considerable success but acknowledging that in the early days he had endured failure and frustration and that, even now, he was often baffled by individual cases but refused to give up. What a breath of fresh air! What an encouragement!

Third, his asides on the tapes revealed him to be a man free from any personal pride or arrogance—a man unimpressed by himself and enjoying the free grace of God. I liked what I heard very much.

Providentially (and to my great delight) within six months we met in London. A colleague arranged a meeting between me and John Wimber at his hotel, just before he was to speak at Westminster Central Hall. We talked, and this was the beginning of a growing relationship. At that time I mentioned that I prayed for legs to be lengthened with some success. (I had prayed for Lorrie White's leg, and it grew.) Subsequently, following a visit I made to Los Angeles, it was arranged that John would come to my hometown of Brighton for a healing conference, where five thousand people enjoyed five unforgettable days and where many lives were transformed.

It was at this conference that I went forward with hundreds of other pastors to be prayed over for empowering for ministry. When John prayed, I felt the presence of God as never before. Waves of power overwhelmed me as, for the first time, I fell to the ground under the influence of the Holy Spirit. Ed Piorek, a Vineyard pastor from California, prayed and prophesied over me with great effect. I lay there "drunk" for what seemed ages. I had previously arranged to take John out to lunch on that day, but he assured me that I was not going to drive him anywhere while I was in *that* condition!

After that experience I had a new faith and expectation that God would come when I ministered to people in prayer and preaching. God's personal love for *me* was more real, more intimate, than I had ever known it to be. This latter effect—that of knowing and being known by my heavenly Father—was the center of his work in me that day. I received fresh courage and faith to pray boldly for people.

South Africa Revisited

Almost immediately after the conference I once again flew to South Africa, this time eager to put into practice what I had recently learned and experienced. At first all did not go well. In South Africa, evening church gatherings are dismissed much earlier than in England. I was unaware of this, so when I wanted to begin praying for people, they all wanted to go home to bed. But after I understood what was happening, I adjusted the schedule to allow for the earlier dismissal at our Capetown meetings. After one or two frustrations at meetings in other major cities, I again arrived at Capetown. At the end of a large celebration I invited the Holy Spirit to come on the people. After a brief pause God moved powerfully among us. Some were healed and many were manifestly filled with the Holy Spirit. One phoned us the next day to say that some had been drunk in the Spirit all night. The following evening at Stellenbosch eclipsed even the Capetown meeting; several were healed, shaken, and filled with the Holy Spirit and many laughed uncontrollably as wave after wave of the power of the Holy Spirit seemed to cross the room.

At home we still feel we have much to learn. We have known glorious manifestations of the Spirit's power including some notable healings, such as the healing of a teenager in the church who had, from birth, lived with the limitations of tunnel vision. One evening two of our young men prayed for him and instantly his vision opened out to a full, normal span. Several others have been physically or emotionally healed and some have been physically "bounced" around the room.

One particular prayer meeting was memorable. We were praying as a church for a team of our young people who were to be involved in an evangelistic program, asking that the Holy Spirit might equip them for the task. As we prayed several of them were powerfully affected. They then turned to pray for the rest of us and, once again, God came with electrifying impact. Several fell under the power of God and some were quite violently shaken. One young man was vigorously bouncing on the floor like a recently landed fish. His physical contortions defied imitation by natural means. His life has taken on a new radiance ever since that evening.

Brighton Conference

More recently, at John's second major conference in Brighton, I was invited to take seminars and, at the conclusion of each, there were powerful manifestations of the Spirit's presence. A local team who worked with me moved out effectively, helping those who came forward for ministry and bringing incisive words of knowledge.

Now a number of people in our church are attending special seminars to follow through the implications and impact of John's visits. There is more expectation of God's intervention than ever before, though we feel we have much to learn and are often disappointed. Many other churches with which I work are similarly encouraged and experiencing more of the power of God, resulting in increasingly fruitful evangelism.

Although in the United Kingdom we have yet to witness the sort of blessing that several other nations are enjoying (for example, Korea, Argentina, Indonesia, and Nigeria), we are nevertheless beginning to see greater numbers of people converted and added to the church. We believe that power evangelism flowing from restored New Testament church life is the answer to our generation, and we are believing God for church growth that will make people sit up and take notice.

We long to reach the nation with the gospel and believe we have a commission from God. In the last eight years our congregation in Brighton has grown from fifty people to just over one thousand. Other churches with which I work (currently about fifty) are enjoying similar proportional growth. The reasons for the growth include, among other factors, a fresh anointing and empowering of the Holy Spirit for personal evangelism. Many of our churches' healing teams pray for the sick regularly and see many people healed. The word is out that God's healing power is real, and people are drawn to that.

As we approach the 1990s we are praying and working toward building large churches that will reach out effectively into Great Britain, Europe, and the ends of the earth. God has promised his Son "Ask of me and I will give you the nations as your inheritance and the ends of the earth as your possession" (Ps. 2:8). It is our intention to equip the saints for works of ministry so that, through the church, that promise shall be fulfilled.

11

Come, Holy Spirit

Mike Flynn

Mike Flynn is rector of St. Jude's Episcopal Church, Burbank, California. He and his wife, Linda, have four children.

It was in the very middle of the middler year of seminary that I was first filled with the Holy Spirit. I was in a real slump: seminary hadn't made me "holy" and I was disappointed and embarrassed that I had expected it to; the initial excitement of entering seminary was long over; graduation looked an eternity away; and I was stewing. One morning in chapel it all came to a head as the service droned on. The upshot was that I decided to quit. I'm not sure exactly what or how much I quit—surely seminary, perhaps my marriage, probably religion—because I never had a chance to find out, for when I went up to the altar rail for Communion, something unbidden, unexpected, and alarming happened when the priest put the bread in my hand. Suddenly something like electricity began happening in me.

I didn't have much time to ponder that for, as the other priest bearing the cup came closer, the sensation increased dramatically. When he was giving the cup to the person next to me, it was nearly unbearable and extremely alarming. The only reason I didn't bolt and run was shyness. As he touched the cup to my lips, the whole business climaxed: I felt as though a Vesuvius of sorts was spewing straight out of the top of my head; I was certain that I was emitting a brilliant white light and that everybody was gawking at me; and my insides were riot with that electric sensation.

I managed to get back to my pew, bury my head in my arms, and sneak a look to see who was looking at me. Wonder of wonders! Nobody was looking at me. I had escaped notice. But then I began to try to sort out what had occurred. The next day I went to the priest who had been handling the cup.

"What happened yesterday?" I asked.

"Where?"

"In chapel, at the altar rail."

"I don't know what you are talking about."

When I told him what I had perceived, he allowed as how people sometimes get mystical experiences once or so in their lives and. . . . He wound down with nothing else to say. I also didn't know what had happened. I did know that I had been touched by God and immediately gave up the idea of quitting. In fact, I used to go to chapel, sit in the same place, and make the same internal decision to try to get it to happen again. Gradually I parked the experience in a corner, going on with my life unaware that there was divine power available for my needs.

Seven years and seven months later, in 1972, I was pastoring a small Episcopal church in El Monte, California. I had been deeply involved in sensitivity training and related behavioral science disciplines. I was something of a radical, I suppose, joining an effort to unionize the clergy; I was a marcher on college campuses, had been arrested, and was proud of it; I was cynical; I was antiestablishment; I was in moral decay. And I was desperately looking for a way out of what I called the "fossil" of the parish (I wasn't picking on my congregation: I thought all parishes were fossils).

Nine O'Clock in the Morning

I had achieved the first of two levels of professional accreditation as a consultant for churches and non-profit organizations, and was ready to obtain the second. I wanted to help churches with planning, staff problems, and organizational difficulties. I had fantasized that with that accreditation I would land consulting jobs that would permit me to leave the parish. In fact, there was a conference in Ohio that I had plane tickets for; I really hoped to make the contacts there that would eventuate in consulting jobs. The day before I was to leave for Ohio, the phone rang and I was cancelled for lack of space.

I plummeted into a deep depression, barely managing to get through church services the next day. The following day, a Monday, one of my parishioners came to my office door to ask me to read a book his married son had pushed off on him. I tossed it on the corner of my desk and went on with my depression. But the next day as I entered my office, that book caught my attention. I decided I might as well get it off my agenda, so I sat down to read *Nine O'Clock in the Morning* by Dennis Bennett.

As I read, I became aware of a sensation in my insides that was barely perceptible. I couldn't figure out what it was. It was like catching a whiff of a favorite dish but still being unable to identify the dish. Also, two opposing reactions were crunching together within me: first, I hated what seemed to me to be an undesirable emotional experience that the book was talking about; second, I was absolutely ravenous for the quality of relationship with God that the book described. And all the time there was this growing sensation, still unidentified after several hours of reading.

At some point, I was presented with a choice. I remember saying something like, "All right, if it takes being an emotional idiot to get that relationship with God, then so be it." Some moments after that I suddenly remembered! It was that thing that had happened to me those years before at the communion rail in the seminary chapel. And as I recalled that experience, the whole thing happened all over again! I knew, and I knew that I knew, that my life had changed. It was August 22, 1972.

The Honeymoon Is Over

Before a week was out, I realized that four major problems in my life had been effortlessly changed: cynicism gave way to hope, a very volatile temper was now easily controlled, long-standing anxiety was replaced with genuine peace, and certain troublesome temptations were quickly defeated. What's more, the parish suddenly became the most exciting place in the world.

Six months later the effortlessness of my new life ended. I was confused, sometimes even doubting that I had been renewed at all. But over time, I was taught by the Holy Spirit that the effortless period was a honeymoon, but that now I had to walk by faith, and faith is work. Nevertheless, I never experienced the depths of personal difficulties that I had before being filled.

Two experiences in my second year in renewal were particularly formative. I got confused about some things and decided to see Mrs. Agnes Sanford about them. After greetings, she came straight to the point. "What do you want me to pray for?" she asked.

Well, my original confusions had clarified themselves somewhat, so I didn't know what I needed prayer for. Agnes said she would pray for me anyway. Standing behind the chair in which I was seated, she forewarned me that she shook when she prayed and that I wasn't to bother about it. So she placed her hands on my head and kept silent a while. Then she prayed that God would give me her anointing for healing of memories (inner healing, as it is called today). I was quite sure that I didn't want an anointing for *that* but was too courteous to tell her that. I drove home thinking the session had been a dead loss.

But a couple weeks later, a woman came into my office, sat down, and explained her serious marriage problems, stemming from spouse abuse. She was in need of the healing of damaged emotions. After a brief argument in my mind with God, I agreed to pray for her. But I realized with a shock that I hadn't the slightest concept of *how* to do it. I had been practicing Christ's presence visually, seeing Jesus on a throne wherever I went. So I looked at Jesus. He got off his throne, knelt down beside the woman, put his right arm around her shoulders, and with his left hand reached right into her heart and pulled out what looked like black jello. This he put into his own heart where it shrank until it evaporated. Then he reached into his own heart again and took out a glob of white jello, which he carefully inserted into the woman's heart where the darkness had been. Finally he turned to me and said, "Do that." I felt rather foolish, but I described out loud in prayer what I had seen Jesus do, and the woman was rather gloriously and immediately healed. I prayed for hundreds of people over the next few years and trained many others to do it.

The second formative experience occurred in meditation. I was meditating on John 15 when I came to verse 5, which ends, "without me you can do nothing."

"Oh, pshaw! Lord, I've done all kinds of things without you," I replied.

"Name one," he challenged.

I sputtered that I could name hundreds, but he said, "one will do."

So I mentioned an event I had led while in sensitivity training that had turned out quite nicely. Immediately I experienced revelation. A horn of plenty, right in front of me, flipped out three pictures of the event I had mentioned. The details are unnecessary here, but it's enough to say that those pictures devastated my estimate of what I had done without him.

Well, he had thrown down the gauntlet. So, for the next six months, whenever I was driving the car and therefore available for ruminating, I went over my whole life looking for things I had done on my own, without him. I came up with five items. So I said, "I'm ready to go up against you on John 15:5 again." Each item was met with that horn of revelatory plenty; he just blew them all to smithereens.

I was so shaken that I went into my office and sat down. "What's going on?" I asked. Then, before my eyes was a 5-inch ruler, which also had a bulb, like a thermometer. The line went up to 5¼ inches and the Lord said to my mind, "Maybe if you ever mobilized all your capabilities, you could produce that much good." The tone was sarcastic. Then the line went up to 5⅜ inches and he said, "And a better man than you could produce that much good." I didn't know how much that was, but I was only saluting at that point.

Then a ruler that went from the foundation of the earth to the highest heaven appeared before me. At eye level, it was at the millions-of-inches mark. And he said, "If you will acknowledge that 'without me you can do nothing,' I will give you my value scale," which was there before my eyes.

"You're on!" I said aloud.

Six weeks later I was aware that a change had been occurring in my insides without knowing what it was. Suddenly it dawned on me what it was: a lifelong inferiority complex had evaporated! I went into church and praised him for about an hour before it occurred to me to ask the cause. He said it was the episode over John 15:5. I rejoiced to praise him that he had lent me his worth to settle the issue of my acceptability.

These two experiences showed me much about the business of trying to collaborate with the living God. No one deserves an anointing. If God sovereignly gives one, he sovereignly gives one. He alone is capable. Part of his capability is to be capable through the likes of us, and that is a great wonder.

Wonderful and Terrible Years

Well, the next eleven years were wonderful-terrible. The wonder was the new life that I knew was available to the whole world. The terrible was how inadequate I was to present this life so that more would take it. All the time, the Lord was teaching me, slowly maturing me, keeping me going. But, to be honest, I was becoming disillusioned. I didn't know if *I* was the problem or if the people were or what. Long periods went by without a single physical healing, which I took as some kind of standard of failure. I was much more effective outside my congregation than within it, which puzzled and upset me. There was frequently the nagging doubt about whether I was fully surrendered to him.

Finally, after feeling that I had failed to renew my parish, I accepted a call to my current parish, glad for a fresh start. When I had been here two years, I was no closer to renewing this church than the previous one, and despair was nipping at my heels. I felt led to take the last Tuesday of each month to go on a prayer retreat. On one of these I was atop the mountain that overlooks Burbank. It was a hard day, for I was in agony over my failure to bring the parish fully alive. As I began to leave the mountaintop to go home, this sentence formed itself in my mind: "No more second-rate Christianity!" It took almost two hours to get back to my car, during which I shouted it, prayed it, cried it, sang it. Within two weeks, things were different in church.

Shortly after that I went to a charismatic pastor's meeting to hear somebody named John Wimmer [sic] speak. He handed out a stack of notes and we went through something called "Building the Church from the Bottom Up." I liked the material, but I didn't care much for the man, for he seemed rather scornful of the historic churches' chances for real vitality. (Later I realized his name was Wimber, when I sent for a copy of the materials to work through more extensively.)

For some reason which I've never been able to recall sufficiently, I decided to buy the first volume of John's healing tapes. Immediately, I was greatly encouraged by a combination of honesty and effectiveness I heard in those tapes. Quickly I bought the other three volumes. I began collecting people at St. Jude's to gather to hear the tapes; and we began trying to "do the stuff," with limited success.

In March of 1984 John taught a healing seminar to about two hundred people from the Episcopal, Presbyterian, and Lutheran churches. There, for the first time as I recall, I saw the Holy Spirit called down. It flat-out blew me away. At the same time people were weeping, laughing, shaking, and praying within yards of each other. I knew, and I knew that I knew, that this wasn't mass hypnosis, emotionalism, charismania, or anything else. This was the Holy Spirit at work. I didn't understand much that was going on, but I knew that it was of God. I didn't *like* a fair bit of what I observed, but I knew that it was the Spirit's doings that I didn't like, so I decided to go with it anyway.

A couple months later I attended a Spiritual Warfare Seminar at the Vineyard. While there, John asked me to accompany him and a small team to Fort Worth. I accepted. And there, in a Baptist church in Fort Worth, I ministered powerfully, if clumsily, in this newfound power of the Holy Spirit.

Taking a Risk

From that time on I was hooked. All that remained was for me to call down the Holy Spirit in my own church. I was a bit afraid of the people's reactions if the Holy Spirit did the same things in our church as he did around John, but it was clear to me that I had to invite his presence. So I did a seminar on "Calling Down the Holy Spirit" in December of that year. After teaching for a couple hours, it was time to call him down. I almost backed out, but I was trapped, because I had announced that I would do it. Finally, I told the people to sit down (which was unnecessary for they were already seated) and relax. I think I was really telling myself to relax. Then I mimicked John by saying, "Come, Holy Spirit."

Now I never felt a greater fool in my whole life. That three-word prayer felt ludicrously inept. There followed a long silence, and nothing was happening. In my mind I was telling the Spirit, "You better show up! You better show up!" But there wasn't any evidence that he heard me. After a couple minutes, people began to shuffle, open their eyes, and look blankly at me. I was desperate, but my untrained eyes could see no evidence of the Spirit on anyone. Finally I spied one girl who just might have looked a tinge more peaceful than before. It was my only shot. So I went up to her and put my hand over her heart and—again mimicking John—said, "Holy Spirit, I bless your peace on this woman." Immediately the peace on her deepened into a sort of holy joy, and we were off and running! Over the next two hours almost every person there manifested the Spirit in some way and received—and many gave—significant ministry. It was glorious!

From that time on, I encouraged our ministry teams to call the Holy Spirit down on those who came for ministry during our worship services. I called him down during counseling sessions. I called him down on strangers who had stopped to chat. I called him down on my wife, my kids. I called him down during sermons. I called him down during House Church prayer times. I called him down on various groups I had been invited to speak to. I called him down on skid-row people we fed, clothed, and witnessed to.

For the first time in my ministry, there was now a reliable power available to back up teaching. My primary gift is exhortative teaching or teaching for practical application. But so often I had concluded a teaching rather lamely, commending the people to try harder, if more instructedly. But the instruction wasn't enough. And prayer, frankly, had become a way of ending teaching instead of inaugurating ministry.

Now this was all different. It was still scary. It remains scary to this day because you never know what the Spirit is going to do. We're often on new turf; or he does a new thing on old turf. I make many mistakes. For example, I get the idea in my mind that He's going to do such and such, but he does something quite unexpected. Frequently I'm not aware of the thing he *is* doing, still trying to work what I thought was going to happen. Or I'll misinterpret a word of knowledge, only later to realize that I was off course. So it's scary. I'm not in control, which is insecurity incarnate.

Nonetheless—nonetheless!—I'm going to call the Holy Spirit down on those I encounter in ministry situations. Even if I'm clumsy and blind, he manages to bless people more than they would've been blessed had I not called him down on them. And my worst fear, that I would hurt someone by this style of ministry, has not been justified. The Spirit always knows what to do, whether I do or not.

Cooperating with the Holy Spirit

This style of ministry requires the changing of assumptions. Last year sometime, I taught one of the sessions of a class on signs and wonders that the student body at Fuller Theological Seminary sponsored. At the end of the teaching, I called the Spirit down. As my sidekick Lloyd Harris and I got in the car after the event, I joked, "Well, I think I must have lied about twenty-five times tonight." Lloyd laughed, knowing what I meant, for I had uttered words of knowledge about twenty-five times. I don't know how the word of knowledge works in you, but in me it is almost always the merest flick across my inner eye. I like to say that the Spirit speaks in a "whis," which is half a whisper. On an emotional level it *feels* like I'm lying when I utter a word of knowledge. I knew that faith was a matter of will rather than emotions or intellect, but I never assumed that the enemy would contest it with my own emotions. It's a minor, but significant learning.

I'm getting better at collaborating with the Holy Spirit. I've observed that the Spirit does one or more of these four categories of things: convict, heal, anoint, or bless. When I'm ministering to groups, I'm beginning to be able to sense which of the four he wants to do. As I minister to individuals (within those groups or privately), I'm becoming more confident that he can use me to help people. I'm finding that I have to throw out my sense of timing and wait for the Spirit to work in people, not minding long silences if necessary, just hanging in with him and them until it seems the time is over. I know that the Holy Spirit cannot yet do everything he would want through me, but he gets more done than he used to, so I am grateful.

And I'm enjoying a kind of peace I never quite knew before. When I was first filled with the Holy Spirit, I said, "Now I know that I am on the right track for the first time in my ministry." And that was true. Now there is something a bit different. There is a stronger sense of being guided, of walking a particular appointed path, of being a piece fitting into a glorious huge puzzle, of not being quite so tormented by the apparent dead-ends, of new hope. My expectation is that I will be learning to be more effective in seeing, collaborating with, and enjoying the Holy Spirit for a good many years to come.

12

A Power Encounter Worth Laughing About

Murray Robertson

Murray Robertson is senior pastor of Spreydon Baptist Church, Christchurch, New Zealand. He and his wife, Marj, have three children.

"Tonight the Lord is going to call out some of you to be healers and some evangelists," John Wimber's voice echoed around the large auditorium in Auckland, New Zealand, in August 1986 where over two thousand had gathered for a conference on "Signs, Wonders and Church Growth."

I felt stirred within. Evangelism has always been something close to my heart since I came to the Lord at a Billy Graham Crusade in New Zealand in 1959. After studying theology in Scotland in the mid-sixties, my wife, Marj, and I began our ministry in a small, somewhat rundown church in Christchurch. During our first few years at the church we saw large numbers of people come to Christ. However, for the couple of years directly preceding the conference we had gone through a much tougher period. At the conference I felt the need for greater equipping of the Spirit in the area of evangelism.

"Those of you whom the Lord is calling as healers are going to have a sign in your body," John Wimber continued. "When that sign occurs, come to the front and we will pray with you." I watched with some interest as various people began to make their way to the front.

Then suddenly my right hand began shaking quite violently, as though I were holding onto a pneumatic drill.

One of the elders of our church was sitting next to me. "You had better go to the front," he said, seeing what was happening to me. "But it's the wrong gift!" I said. "I want to be effective in evangelism, not healing!" However, I could hardly argue with what was happening to me, so I made my way to the front and was prayed for along with the others who had responded.

God had not finished with me that night. John Wimber continued speaking, "There are some of you here who have been active in ministry for a long time, but you have grown weary and discouraged, and the Holy Spirit is going to come and refresh you." I had a feeling that I wanted to laugh but thought that was hardly appropriate. "The Spirit will come in waves," said Wimber, "each wave catching up more people than the one before." Down the front someone started laughing. Then someone else. This must be the refreshing of the Spirit, I thought—by now no longer able to repress my own desire to laugh.

This sense of joy in the Spirit continued across the auditorium for ten minutes or so, then subsided. Those who had been laughing, stopped—except for me. I found I just could not stop. Neither, after a while, could I stand. I ended up falling over the seats in front, then the row behind, and finally rolling around the floor, holding my sides and roaring with laughter. By now, a knot of spectators was gathering—I must have been providing some good entertainment! Interestingly enough, part of me felt somewhat detached from the whole experience. I knew what was going on—there were months, if not years, of frustration in ministry that were being drained out of me. But I was not aware at the time of the nature of some new things that God was doing inside me.

The laughter went on for about three-quarters of an hour. Then, as it was stopping, a fellow pastor and very good friend of mine put his hand on my head and said, "Lord, give him some more"— which set me off for an additional three-quarters of an hour. By the end of that time, I was pleading with him not to pray for me anymore as my ribs were hurting so much from all the laughing.

The next day, I briefly met John Wimber and told him that my ribs were still hurting from laughing so much. His response was to relate this to the whole conference—adding that I was the first Baptist holy roller he had met!

A Healthy Experience

If I were new to this whole dimension of the Holy Spirit working in power, I would be very tempted, at this point, to turn to the next chapter, hoping for a more sane assessment of the Spirit's work. In hindsight, although what happened to me that night seems a bit bizarre, it felt a very healthy experience and, as someone pointed out to me at the end of it, Acts 2:13 does provide an insight that it had happened before.

Now, six months later, looking back on that night I can see that it proved to be quite a turning point in my own life and in the life of our church. For just over a decade, we had been seeking to be creatively open to the work and gifts of the Spirit in our church, seeking to develop a third option between the Pentecostal churches, on the one hand, and the traditional conservative evangelicals, on the other. We sent teams from our church around New Zealand and Australia sharing a ministry of spiritual renewal in the church. However, we had been sensing that something more was needed. We were no longer seeing the conversions that had occurred in the early years of the renewal. Many of our small groups seemed to be turning inward and there was a spiritual dryness around. For six months prior to the Wimber conference, our pastoral team had been on its knees every week, praying for God to send revival to our midst. So, for us, John Wimber's visit was into a situation that God had been preparing.

Healing

What has happened since? Well, we have seen a very significant development in the healing ministry in the church. For years we had been open to the healing dimension of the Holy Spirit's work; every week at the communion services we invited people to the front for prayer for healing of various kinds. God has honored that over the years but, in the time since August 1986, I sense we have entered a new dimension in this area. We were fortunate that, not only did we have quite a group from our church go up to the conference in Auckland but, the following weekend, we had a visit from Pastor Tom Stipe and a team from the Denver Vineyard, which meant that most of our church was exposed to these particular dimensions of ministry.

Prior to the conference, we had a small team involved every week praying for people's physical healing. In the months since, this ministry has expanded considerably, so that now we have several teams praying with the sick in the course of the week. There has been a much greater development of the gift of the word of knowledge in relation to the healing ministry and the expansion of the dimension of power in praying for both the physically and emotionally sick. I sense what the Holy Spirit has done is to give us a very significant push down a road that we were already traveling and, for this, we can only praise God.

About four weeks after the conference, I was due to leave for Wellington to speak at a weekend camp. Just as I was getting ready to go, the telephone rang. It was the husband of an expectant mother carrying a baby of twenty-two weeks' gestation; he was in tears as his wife had just been admitted to hospital with premature labor. The situation was made worse as she had miscarried only some months previously. At the hospital, one of the doctors had asked her if she wanted an abortion or whether things should be left to run their course.

"I have got a plane to catch," I told him, "but I will get one of the other pastors to call at the hospital." I put the phone down but felt uneasy. "You go to the hospital," the Holy Spirit said to me. So I began praying and saw a picture of a womb with a baby struggling to come out. As I watched, the struggling stopped and the baby calmed down. "We've got to go to the hospital before we leave," I said to Marj. On the way there, I related the vision to her. "It might be too late," she said. "Her husband said the waters have burst and the contractions have started, so it's only a matter of time." We walked into the hospital ward where the husband was sitting alongside his wife in the bed. "We have come to pray for the baby," we said. So for three-quarters of an hour we sat on the edge of the bed, talked to the unborn child, and prayed for Jesus to touch it. Not long after we had begun praying, the mother felt a sensation of power going right through her body. So from that point on, with an increasing sense of joy, we began blessing what God was doing.

We had to leave for the airport. Back at the hospital, an hour went by and the staff came and took the mother for a scan. It was announced that, incredibly, there was ample fluid round the baby. It appeared that the fluid that had been lost had been replaced. "I believe miracles do happen," another doctor said. Months have passed and we are now preparing for a dedication service for a beautifully normal baby who was born at the right time!

Renewed Evangelism

Interestingly enough, as well as the area of healing we have also seen some major developments in the area I was originally most concerned about—that of evangelism. In the months since the conference we have had occasions, both in the worship services and in our prison ministry, when the Holy Spirit has been invited to come onto groups of people and we have seen some hardcore pagans reduced to tears by the Spirit's presence and sovereignly brought into the kingdom of God.

The Sunday afternoon after the Wimber conference, I was praying and asking the Lord what he was wanting to do in our worship that evening. Into my mind came a picture of a man dressed in punk-rock garb, complete with black leather jacket and chains. I must confess that my first reaction was to try and put this out of my mind so I could concentrate on some more pious things God would be wanting to do. However, that evening I shared the picture that had come to me and said that, although the person may not be dressed just like that at the moment, the Lord wanted to tell him that the time had come for his chains to be broken. At the back of the gathering, unknown to me, there was a young man who had been on drugs for twelve years and who had spent several years in prison. As I shared the word, his chest began to heave. "That's me," he said to someone standing by. "What am I supposed to do?" He was brought to the front and introduced to Ted, one of our pastors. He told Ted that ten months previously he had cried out to God in desperation and had come off his drug addiction. He had faith in God but could not accept that Jesus was the Son of God. Something of a theological debate followed about the deity of Christ. When he could see it was going nowhere, Ted, who had also attended the Wimber conference that week, asked him if he could pray with him. As he prayed, the Holy Spirit came on the young man and he began to shake. "How do you feel now?" Ted asked him.

"Great," was the reply.

"What do you want to do now?"

"I want to ask Jesus into my life!" he said.

This certainly is an improvement on the pleading and, in some cases, the manipulation that we have often been guilty of in evangelical churches in our attempts to get people into the kingdom. Increasingly we are trying to encourage our people to pray with non-Christian friends with needs and see the way that God touches their lives.

Hearing from God

One of the things that impressed me about John Wimber's ministry was the sense of hearing from God about what he was wanting to do in a situation before any ministry was undertaken. This is an area of ministry in which I have felt particularly challenged and stretched in the months that have followed. I think, like many of us in ministry, I have a strong tendency to step into a situation and make assumptions about what God is wanting to do, rather than spend the time waiting to hear.

One of the most interesting experiences of hearing from God in the months that have followed the Wimber conference took our whole family to Hong Kong for about six weeks over Christmas and New Year. Jackie Pullinger and a team of Chinese brothers from Hong Kong had come to our church for a missions convention about a month after the Wimber conference. It was interesting hearing from her how much her own ministry had taken a new turn as a result of John Wimber's ministry. It was even more interesting hearing about Hong Kong and the situation where more addicts and other lost souls were wanting to come to the Lord than they had people to pray. I felt extremely challenged by this.

After they had gone, the Holy Spirit began speaking to Marj and me. We had been starting to make plans for our summer holidays here in New Zealand, but God was making it quite clear to us that we were to go to Hong Kong and take our three high-school-aged children plus a couple of others from our church with us. Naturally it was going to cost a lot of money we didn't have, but I felt that, if this were right, the Lord would provide the money without our having to make the financial need known to anyone. And he did.

The whole time in Hong Kong turned out to be a very stimulating experience. It was a real privilege being involved in ministry with the people there and it turned out that we arrived at a very crucial time for their work. I have rarely had such a sense of being in the right place at the right time and it has challenged me very deeply about the needs of a place like Hong Kong and the possibilities of multiplying churches empowered by the Holy Spirit among the masses of the poor. On top of all that, it turned out to be a spiritual high point in the lives of our family members as well. It highlighted for me the importance of listening to God for unusual and important kinds of guidance. I don't think any of our family will ever be the same again.

Another area of hearing something from the Lord has been with our home group ministry. I think our situation is similar now to that of many churches in the Western world that have sustained home groups for a long period. A decade ago we felt that the Lord was telling us to let all the programs and activities of the church die so that the church could be reborn around small groups. In the last few years we have developed this further by starting new Sunday morning congregations out of clusters of home groups. However, the home groups were becoming stale. There comes a limit to the amount of deep personal sharing you can do year after year with the same people if you are not in a growing group.

In the light of the new things we were sensing the Holy Spirit was beginning to do in the church, I felt the right thing to do was to call all the home group leaders together and simply pray and listen. The Lord spoke to us very strongly prophetically. He was getting tired of our investing all our energies in loving each other when there was a world out there that he loved with great compassion. He was wanting to do something new in our midst. He would rebuild our small group ministry around groups who would love and care for others, particularly the poor and needy.

We felt the message was very clear and we knew we should take the step of closing our whole home group ministry so that the Spirit could give birth to something new. It is one thing to do that in a small church, but it's something different when there are many hundreds involved in groups with a vested interest in carrying on. But, with precious few murmurs, the whole church is gathering together to pray and to allow God to rebirth something new in our midst. Already we are seeing numbers of groups emerging with specific ministries to different kinds of people. We do not want to throw away the very valuable insights of a decade of close supportive, caring relationships, but we are seeing already that these relationships must express themselves in mission where God's heart is—among the poor.

Missionary Heart

Over the past decade, we have seen the Lord grow a real missionary heart in the church for Asia, for the poor and, recently, more specifically for the urban poor in Asia's big cities. What concerned me was the growing gulf existing between them and those living at ease back in New Zealand. Now the Holy Spirit is closing the gap and thrusting increasing numbers of us into mission among the poor at home.

While some people in the church may find it a bit unnerving to be told we are not precisely sure where we are going but we are going to pray about it, it is certainly better than sitting around a table arguing together about where God is wanting to take the church—which tragically is the model for guidance that too many of us are still locked into.

One final comment. I think the thing about John Wimber that impressed me the most was that he came across to me as a man who was not driven. Now, I don't know him personally, so it could just be that he is just a better actor than the rest of us. However, I could not help feeling that the lack of a sense of drivenness was related to his commitment to the sovereignty of God in healing and evangelism. I have never had any problem with this as a theological proposition, but I am not sure how much difference it has made to the way I have behaved as a church leader.

I sense that, since the night I made a spectacle of myself on the carpet in Auckland, I am becoming more relaxed within, with I hope a greater willingness to give God the space to do what he wants to do in our midst. But then I suspect that that is what the ministry is supposed to have been about all along.

13

Recovering the Ministry I Left Behind

Tom Stipe

Tom Stipe is senior pastor of the Vineyard Christian Fellowship, Denver, Colorado, which numbers four thousand. He has traveled throughout the United States, England, South Africa, New Zealand, and Australia ministering as an evangelist, church consultant, and pastoral trainer. He and his wife, Maryellen, have two children.

My religious roots are twofold. I think I honestly met the Lord when I was nine years old. I was little Southern Baptist boy living with my grandma and grandpa prior to my adoption. I should probably mention at this point that the first nine years of my life were less than ideal. I moved from parent to stepparent, to aunts and uncles, to grandparents, and after a myriad of changes from town after town and school after school, I was adopted into the Stipe family. I remember the night I went forward to receive Jesus in a service specifically designed for children. After I was adopted, I was raised a Methodist in a southern California church that had a tremendous amount of spiritual diversity. There were leaders who had a personal relationship with Christ as well as those who did not. Some were evangelical while others were liberal to the point of denying that a personal relationship with Jesus was possible today.

As a result, I did not hear a clear presentation of the gospel that depicted Jesus as Savior and that required a life decision until I was a senior in high school. As it turned out, there was an undercover evangelical who became the church's Christian education director in charge of youth. Ken Working was a graduate of Fuller Theological Seminary. Behind the scenes, Ken began to work on me at the level of my commitment to Jesus.

At the time, I was experiencing a lot of trouble as a teenager at home. I had a strong commitment to my social life. Staying out all night with the boys was more important to me than repentance. I didn't see myself as a non-Christian, because I had been at church every Sunday for most of my life. The experience that I had at age nine led me to believe that I did not qualify for what Ken was trying to tell me I had to do.

Ken had a friend who was a youth director in Walnut Creek, California. At the time, he had one of the largest youth groups in the country. I was introduced to Ron Richie, who eventually went on to be an associate at Peninsula Bible Church in northern California. Ken had asked Ron and a couple of his teenagers to come and share their testimonies at our southern California church. At that meeting, I heard a young man give his public testimony concerning his life with Christ.

As it turned out we were both seventeen. He had experienced some significant trouble in his home life and in his childhood. After the meeting, I sought him out to see if he was for real. I cornered him in a room and began a thorough interrogation. He gave me a basic four-point presentation about Jesus, but I wanted to know more. Every time he wanted to expand the issues of sin and repentance, I would move him back to a previous point in his spiel, the "God loves you and has a wonderful plan for your life" part. At the time, I did not perceive myself as a sinner in need of repentance. But, one thing I did know, my life was miserable and I saw no immediate hope for my future as a youth or an adult.

The part of the witness that caused me to listen was centered on a sense of a future and a promise of destiny; it was like opening a time capsule that was implanted in me when I accepted Jesus as a child. When my newfound friend was talking about his life in Christ, I wanted to know more about what he meant. I drilled him for about three hours until I was sure that what he was talking about in public was real in private.

My situation at home continued to deteriorate. My relationship with my parents continued to be strained. Ken contacted my parents because they were preparing to make some permanent arrangements for me to live under state supervision. You might say I was a rough kid to raise! Ken suggested that he make arrangements for me to stay with a Christian family in northern California instead.

The result of this move produced a totally new living environment. The Christian family I moved in with helped me to understand and respond to what God was doing in my life. They opened their hearts and home to me. Going to their church was an experience that allowed me to see effective preaching, teaching, and evangelism at work. I took my first steps toward living the life of a believer. I became involved in a coffee house ministry, witnessing, and high-school Bible study groups. My early Baptist and Methodist roots began to pay off. What was planted in me so many years before began to grow.

It was during this time that I first became aware that I was truly and clearly called to the ministry. I remember one day outside the gymnasium at Walnut Creek Presbyterian Church when the Spirit of the Lord encountered me. I can picture the spot and the moment. I could not explain this for a number of years, but I knew that the Lord said, "I've called you to preach the gospel to thousands." At that moment, I started looking at life through a different set of lenses. I began to see people as objects of God's love rather than people to be taken advantage of.

Beware of the Bean Field!

After things smoothed out at home, I returned to southern California and graduated from high school. I looked for the nearest Bible college, applied, and was accepted. It was a Church of Christ Bible college. Thus my influences to that point were Baptist, Methodist, Presbyterian, and now Church of Christ. After a year in college, I was hired as a Methodist youth director in the Orange county area of southern California. My pastor was a closet charismatic who believed in healing and tongues but had to camouflage these activities in the course of daily church life.

In addition to being in charge of the youth department, I was the assistant leader of a local Campus Life group. One night, in the home where our group was meeting, our leader took me to the side and said, "Listen! This is a warning! There is a little church over next to a bean field in Costa Mesa that you need to keep your kids away from. They raise their hands and speak in tongues. If any of your kids get caught up in it, try and get them out."

"What else do they do?" I asked.

"They sing for an hour and people fall down when they claim to be filled with the Spirit, plus they say they see healings."

"Well, what else do they do?" I asked.

"They sing rock and roll music to Jesus and have a wild preacher," he responded.

I was there the next night, and so was Jesus in presence and power. I knew it was the Lord. I saw some things that I had never seen before, but I knew it wasn't a performance. I saw the power of God in ways that I had only heard about; the kingdom of God was present. I had not known that since the day I became a believer. I thought that you get born again, feel Jesus, and then the rest of your walk is by faith; I was taught that you never go by feelings anymore after that initial experience. Too much of the presence of God was condemned as unhealthy for the intellect.

This place was somehow very different. I sensed the presence and the love of God. Maryellen—then my girlfriend, now my wife—and I went again the next week. We sat on the floor in the back. It was packed and the Lord was there again! People were saved by the dozens and filled with the Holy Spirit in a powerful way—a way that I knew was not being generated by the people themselves or a youth leader's manual.

Two weeks later my curiosity led me to take about ten members of my youth group. They were all born again, but that night they had hands laid on them and they were filled with the Holy Spirit and spoke in tongues. (This is not meant as a theological statement; it is simply the way I saw it occur.) A few weeks later it was my turn to have youth Sunday at the church where I was youth director. This was my responsibility twice annually. We were given the whole church service. Because so many of the young people were on fire for the Lord at that time, I asked several to give their testimonies. One by one they gave testimony about what had happened to them at this other church. I was in trouble from that moment on and was eventually fired from that position. When this happened, I made a decision to involve myself in the activities of Calvary Chapel, Costa Mesa, and the Jesus movement.

The Jesus Movement

These were marvelous years of seeing thousands come to know Jesus. I first became involved with the house movement. There were various Christian houses that young people moved into communally. Under a complex pastoral structure, we shared rooms in a large house, witnessed for Jesus, shared meals together, and had nightly Bible studies. I also became involved in the mainstream of the musical phenomenon that was taking place in what was beginning to be called "the Jesus movement."

After weeks of attending church nightly, I began developing a personal liturgy. We would worship most of the time, sometimes a cappella; a few soloists and sometimes groups like "Love Song" would come and sing and further lead us in worship. One of the pastors or evangelists would come and teach out of the Bible. God would then begin working all over the room—saving, filling, and healing. I remember sitting at the back and negotiating with God, wondering if I had not become somewhat ambitious in my newfound joys. I remember saying, "Lord, if it's okay with you, I want to do both of these things. I want to preach and I want to sing. I want to play music for you and I want to present the gospel."

Within a few days I got a couple of other guys together and began to write songs. For the next several years I was privileged to be involved in the mainstream of the evangelism and the music that came out of Calvary Chapel. Eventually I became a staff member. I taught regular Bible studies and spoke at evangelistic concerts. The Lord had answered my prayer. At the Saturday night Maranatha Concerts, we played and preached to thousands every week. Tens of thousands of young people came to know Jesus during those years.

I toured the United States with the contemporary Christian music groups "Country Faith" and "Wing and a Prayer," the latter of which was a regrouping of the well-known band "Love Song." We played to capacity crowds at Knotts Berry Farm and the World's Fair in Spokane, Washington. I also worked as a record producer for Maranatha Music, a music ministry and record company born during my days at Calvary Chapel. I produced several albums for Maranatha Music as well as for Pat Boone. The most notable production for the latter was the first "Boone Girls" record, which featured Pat's daughter, Debbie Boone.

For five years I also watched the Lord work in what we called "afterglows," which were services held immediately after the main service or concert. In these afterglows we would pray for the sick and pray for the people to be filled with the Holy Spirit. With great power the Lord would come to heal—cancer, tumors, deafness, and other illnesses. Each time we gathered we were in the classroom of the Spirit.

Rocky Mountain High

Though I was involved in one of the fastest growing churches in America, the Lord spoke clearly to Maryellen and me to move to Colorado to start a church in the Denver area. When we moved we supported ourselves the first six months through the activity of my ongoing music ministry—concert events, involvement with music groups, and record production. We started the church basically with the dynamic of Bible teaching at the forefront. I had been trained well and had become competent in presenting scriptural truth due to the strong commitment of Calvary Chapel to Bible teaching. This and the responsibility of speaking or singing several times a week to thousands made me more than confident as a would-be church plant-er. With the blessing of my pastor, friends, and family along with prayers that Jesus would go ahead of us, it was pack the truck and off to Colorado we go.

After a few months of working, making new friends, and getting settled in, we started a Sunday afternoon Bible study and invited a few friends to join us. The format was simple—a little singing, Bible study, fellowship, and prayer. It seemed to be very functional; more and more people were attracted and stayed until the basement of our house was packed. From there we moved to a small Baptist fellow-ship hall. There we began to hold music events in addition to our Bible studies. People turned out in droves for the music events but didn't seem interested in staying and becoming involved in our church. After two years of struggles, a hundred Saturday events and Sunday Bible studies later, we had managed to draw and keep about 150 people. After my years of success as a public speaker, this felt like failure to me. I became very disillusioned. After all, I was an evangel-ist, wasn't I?

My personal frustration had risen to be point that I had returned to southern California and asked for my old job back at Calvary Chapel. I also attempted to secure a staff position with a friend of mine in Sacramento. Both avenues of escape led to a dead end. I returned home in a swirl of self-doubt. I was trying to answer a question popu-lar with pastors and church planters these days, "What am I doing wrong?"

My best friend at that time was Chuck Fromm, the director of Maranatha Music. On more than one occasion, he had an available shoulder to cry on. This time when I shared with him my woes, he responded by driving me to meet John Wimber at his home in Yorba Linda. The introduction was brief, but the agenda I had brought along was not. We began to discuss my situation. I felt closer to God now than I ever had before, but the results of our ministry in Denver were not the results that we had envisioned after being stirred to go there. I was preaching, teaching, evangelizing, and meeting dozens of new people a week. However, I saw people come in and out of the church with no measurable level of commitment. After a couple of hours of intense listening, John wagged his head a couple of times, rose from his chair while mumbling a few words about infrastructure, and disappeared into his hall closet.

Brown-Bagging It

After a few minutes of wondering what was going on, my curiosity got the better of me and I followed him to the closet. He was filling two brown paper bags—one with hundreds of pages of notes and the other with dozens of cassette tapes. He handed me both brown paper bags filled to the brim with material from Pete Wagner, Chuck Kraft, himself, and others from Fuller Seminary. It wasn't bound, there was no artwork, just brown paper sacks filled with church growth material. I instantly became a seminary student.

A couple of months later I saw John again and he gave me two more brown bags filled with more class study information from the Fuller Church Growth Department. I was introduced to the basics of celebration, congregation, cell, and infrastructure. John came to Denver and helped me train my first ten small-group leaders. I was beginning to add building blocks to the foundation. As a result of this and other forms of leadership training, the church began to grow. In fact, at one particular point, John sensed the synergism that was building in the church and told me that if I would start ten more groups, the church would double in the next five months. I said, "How do you measure that?" He just smiled and said, "I'll tell you later. Just do it and see what happens." Sure enough, we did and four months later the church had doubled. I was excited about church growth!

We grew to about thirteen hundred people counting both adults and children. We were still renting facilities from schools and other churches. I was happy. With thirteen hundred people in my church I was seen as a success with my peers. I was invited to prayer breakfasts. I was accepted at pastors' conferences. I was beginning to grow content with what we had accomplished. I was pleased and appreciative for all that had happened.

That Messy Power Stuff

It was at that time that the Lord began to speak to me about his power again. In my history I had not only been exposed to the dynamics of the Jesus movement, but I had taken the opportunity to work with people such as Katherine Kuhlman who had also known the power of God. The Spirit of God began to nudge me with questions like, "Why don't you lay hands on people anymore? Why don't you pray for the sick? Why don't you allow tongues and interpretation? What about prophecy?" I had simply found them to be too messy to add to my tools for church planting and growth. It was inconvenient and seemed to take a constant effort to explain the value and place of many of these gifts. It was too embarrassing to deal with out-of-line or off-the-wall prophecies. I found it embarrassing and unnecessarily risky to lay hands on people and not know if they would be filled with the Spirit and/or speak in tongues. My fear of not knowing if this would work had simply caused me to abandon a section of my practice that had birthed my ministry.

I believed in it; I had a theology for it, but not a practice. I believed in the fullness of the Spirit. I believed in the power of God. I believed in all the things that I had seen—the falling, the shaking, and the tongues. I knew it to be a life-changing experience, but when I moved to Colorado, it was almost as though I used the opportunity to just drop off the things I didn't like about the movement of the Spirit and simply lead a Bible church. A unique mixture of preaching, Bible teaching, evangelism, and church growth was enough for me but was not enough for God.

A Breakfast Appointment

One early morning, the day after Mother's Day, I awoke about five AM to a very strong impression: call John Wimber; he needs to know that everything is okay! I first thought that this was just my emotions; perhaps I was missing my newfound friend and colleague. As I paced the floor for another hour the impression grew stronger—call John and encourage him. All of these inner thoughts seemed simple and in my mind I thought them to be unnecessary. After all, John was the one who encouraged; how could I be an encouragement to him? After a few more minutes I dialed the phone expecting to hear a sleepy if not irritated "Hello."

John had been awake all night. He had been pillaging his enormous library to discover some historical reference for what had happened in his church the night before. On that Sunday evening, he had asked an old colleague of mine from the Jesus movement to speak. After a brief testimony my old colleague prayed what is considered by many to be a simple closing benediction. He prayed for the Spirit of God to come. The difference was that, rather than ending the service, this prayer began the ministry of the Holy Spirit.

John began to describe the works of the Spirit he had seen that evening. My memory banks were jolted. I saw a clear picture of everything that had happened—the power, the healing, masses of otherwise normal people falling under the hand of God; the wide-eyed observers and the shocked and anxious staff. With a tone of great expertise, I said to John, "Don't worry, it's the Lord. It is the stuff the Jesus movement was made out of." With each descriptive detail from John, I confirmed that these events would bring great health to the church.

In the midst of these statements to John, I was struck deep in my heart. I had seen no such works of the Spirit in my own church since the day I had started. At one point, John sensed my reminiscence and asked me what was wrong. As the tears began to well up, I confessed that what I was confirming to be a great blessing to him was in fact an enormous void in my own life and ministry.

The Hunter and the Hunted

As the weeks passed I continued to sense a deepening conviction about the ministry of power I had left behind. It was during this period that John again, excited and hungry to know more about the power of God and its effect on the growth of the church, gave me a call. He had heard about some of the great works that God was doing in South Africa and had responded to an invitation to go and minister. He saw this as an opportunity to learn and experience more and said, "We are taking a group to South Africa to minister. Why don't you come along?" My first response to the invitation was, "No, it's too expensive. I can't afford it and it isn't convenient. And anyway I've got a hunting trip planned; I simply don't want to go." John was excited about the things he had been hearing, reading, and seeing. He was hungry for the things of the Spirit. As he shared with me, I took on a sort of "Yeah, I know all about that stuff; you go ahead. I have things to do. Have a good time in South Africa." I went into the Rockies on my preplanned hunting trip while John and his group went to South Africa.

What happened to me while hunting can only be described in my understanding as a visitation. The Spirit of the Lord came to me in the most fearsome way that I could ever describe. Once I was alone, the Spirit began to bring up some of the areas of conviction that he had been speaking to me about and in a very stern way. As the severity increased, I began to doubt that it was God at all and began to believe that it was an attack from the enemy. As this feeling of fear and loneliness increased, I began to think that I had accidentally stumbled onto an Indian burial ground and was under the attack of demons. I felt that God was a thousand miles away.

I had never been without his presence. I thought that his grace, kindness, and his favor was lifting from me. As I look back, I realize that what the Lord was doing was allowing me to feel what it was like to be without him. To feel the loneliness, the insanity, the lack of salvation. I realized at that moment that I would probably have not been alive if it had not been for the Lord. I felt as though the Lord was saying, "Are you going to serve me? I saved your life. If you are not going to serve me, I may as well take you home." I was convinced at that moment that if I had not recommitted my ministry to the Lord, I would not have come down from that mountain.

The presence of the Lord was so fearsome that I realized that he had saved me to serve and not to convenience myself. The real issue was, if you're done, you're all done. If you are all finished serving me and obeying me, then you're all done and I may as well take you home to be with me. My first thought was, "Where is that kind of experience in the Bible?" It didn't take long for me to find that with Moses the issue of obedience was so significant that God had threatened his life. It was a time of negotiation in which I realized that I had fulfilled the biblical possibilities and had ignored Paul's warnings. I had quenched, denied, and despised the Holy Spirit.

From Belief to Practice

All of this further developed and diagnosed the problem of an incredible gap between my theology and practice. I recalled the story of Peter and Paul in Galatians. Peter had been involved in the supernatural; he was there on the day of Pentecost. He had seen the crippled man healed. He had been delivered from the hands of death by an angel. He had a supernatural vision that led him to the house of Cornelius. God had revealed to him that there was no difference between the Gentiles and him. Peter had his theology forged by God himself. But, in Galatians, we are told that he had forgotten to practice what he knew to be from God. I saw myself in that. I had had the benefit of seeing it all—the great men and women of God, great healers, great Bible teachers, great evangelists—and had simply chosen to neglect the power of the Spirit. I began to realize what my mountain experience was all about.

I had grown very content. Thirteen hundred people spelled success. I could pay all the bills. I could travel the world if I wanted to. I was respected. I had a good salary and an adequate staff. The church was at a very comfortable size. I had no intention of taking any more risks than necessary.

From that point forward, the Lord began to add a sweetness to our worship. I didn't say anything publicly right away to the church. It was something God was doing to me. I wasn't in a hurry to broker my experience because I didn't know how to deal with it. First of all, I had to theologize it. Second, I had to discover what practical application there was for me and the church I pastored.

During all the contemplation, the one thing I did know to do, which was common to all that I had seen in a power ministry, was to worship. So as a fellowship we began to worship longer and with greater intensity. The power of God came to such a degree that sometimes it became difficult to preach. The more we worshiped, the more power. The more power, the better I taught.

Give Me Back My Church—Our Own Mother's Day Miracle

One Mother's Day during my final early morning preparation, the Lord said, "Are you going to give me the church back?" It struck me as odd because my focus was on something else. I just said, "Yes, Lord, you do whatever you want today. You can have it. Whatever you want to do is okay with me." It seems I had become very cooperative after the showdown on that fateful day in the mountains. I thought that the Lord was making this an issue, because whenever there were special holidays, I knew that guests would be present. You want to have the cleanest, sharpest service you can. It was toward the end of worship and we were just praising the Lord and his sweetness was there again. Suddenly a woman sitting on an aisle seat jumped out into the aisle shuddering and praising God. My first thought was that this was someone who was going to subject us to a Pentecostal outburst. But I recognized that the tears were sincere. I did not know what else to do but to call her forward. A few weeks before, she had fallen and broken several bones on the left side of her body. She had been placed in traction. Her family had taken her out of traction so that she could come and see her first granddaughter be dedicated to the Lord. When God's power fell on her, she jumped out of her seat. The Lord dramatically and dynamically healed her in front of the whole church. I was so amazed that I didn't preach or take up the offering. I kept thinking, "If this is what it means to give God's church back to him, I'm in BIG trouble. Nobody will come back next week." While I was dealing with all of this, the Lord showed me a picture of the church that I still use today.

"The church is a hospital!" I thought to myself as I was renegotiating with God. "If it's not okay to bleed at the hospital, then I'd probably better get out of the hospital business. If it's not all right to get healed at the hospital, then I probably should shut the doors. If there is no emergency room or no ambulance service for going and getting people who need help the worst, then I probably better get out of this business." That day I was the last one to leave. I was sitting in my car and I saw the family of this woman walking across the parking lot hovering around her watching her legs, staring at her walking by herself. Tears were running down all of their faces. I thought, "If this is the result of giving the church back to God, then he can have it."

That was the beginning of a release of the Spirit. I fell back into it quite easily because I knew it was the Lord. I had much to learn in terms of praying for the sick and rebuilding old models. I had to learn to allow time for healing to occur—to invite the Spirit of God to come. But it was as though the Lord so graciously just came and began to do it again—began to minister again.

The following year when the invitation came to go to South Africa, I was the first one to sign up. I began a common pilgrimage along with John Wimber and others in the Vineyard.

The Vineyard Denver

By this time, with our church at about thirteen hundred, we were turning hundreds of people away due to lack of facility. They just couldn't get in and I couldn't add more services because we were meeting in someone else's church facility. This strangulation helped us decide to lease our first building, which was northwest of downtown Denver. When we moved, the church began to grow again. The church more than doubled from thirteen hundred to over three thousand in less than six months. This came, I believe, because I was obedient to what God wanted me to do and where he wanted me to take his people. I believe we have an excellent chemistry for growth and health in the church. It includes a commitment to church planting, a strong commitment to Bible teaching, a practice of church growth principles, a healthy infrastructure, and an ongoing relationship to signs and wonders and the power of God.

V

Missionary Encounters

There are no better candidates for a power encounter than Western missionaries in a non-Christian culture. There are at least three reasons for this. First, if they have not opened themselves fully to God's power, they cannot deal effectively with the spiritual needs of the people—needs that frequently involve demon possession and satanism. Second, the influence of rationalism in Western culture (and in their own lives) is magnified, is most visible when they attempt to function in most non-Western cultures. Missionaries cannot help but feel less spiritual than those they are ministering to! Third, because Pentecostals are the most successful missionaries today, almost all missionaries, even those who deny the supernatural today, have seen power encounters. These are compelling reasons for missionaries to open themselves more fully to God's power and the gifts of the Holy Spirit. When they do, power encounters follow.

14

Laying Aside Regrets

Lorrie White

Lorrie White travels extensively and speaks at a variety of Christian conferences with her husband, John. She served for ten years as a missionary in Latin America. The Whites have five grown children and three grandchildren.

I really cannot remember when it began. I always seemed to have been in contact with the Lord. Even when I was tiny I felt he heard me and we had a relationship. Teaching about Jesus from almost any source powerfully attracted me.

Yet my home in a Nova Scotian village was not a Christian home, although we had goodness, morality, and happiness and we were a close family. My dad and my uncle were commercial fishermen, and my grandfather was the lighthouse keeper. But Sunday school for me was—well, not hated exactly— but certainly *endured*. Something about it didn't taste and smell the same as the Lord.

But Charles E. Fuller did. When I was seven I used to sneak downstairs at night and turn the radio on softly for the Fuller Gospel Hour, crouching in the dark to hear it. I learned all the gospel songs by heart and "went forward" with every invitation, wanting with all my heart to be with Jesus. Yet there was always a sense of incompleteness, of something lacking.

I made my first public "decision" when I was twelve (really, I suppose, a public declaration of a decision made many times over) and then when I was seventeen I made a commitment in public to follow Christ fully. But looking back I sense that the public declarations were outward expressions of a yearning that was never completely satisfied, a yearning for the fullness of Christ. I was drawn by an attraction that never ceased to pull.

New Tribes Mission

I had a Bible and I read it, but the help I received was limited. I had left home to work when I was fifteen, and from Halifax where I got my first job I went on to Boston and attended Park Street Congregational Church. The ministry of Harold Ockenga helped me enormously, but the Bible still did not become really alive. In fact, even when I wound up in Bible school, the Bible itself remained remote. I passed examinations on its contents, because my teachers taught us what the Bible contained. But the teaching, excellent in its way, never opened a door through which I could explore Scripture for myself.

Curiously enough, Scripture came alive a little for me and powerfully for others whenever I tried to teach it to my friends or when I taught it on the mission field. But I can now see that I didn't have much of a handle on it. I went to the Philippines with the New Tribes Mission when I was twenty-three and wound up on the west coast of an island called Palawan, along with another Canadian girl and two Filipino girls.

It was a tough but rewarding assignment among a fairly primitive and unevangelized tribal people. "Why were you so long in coming?" was the question we were asked when we were able to communicate the object of our study. The question simultaneously excited us greatly and grieved us deeply. And God began work in the tribe that continues to this day.

But the primitive life, the treks through jungle, the boat trips were all cut short for me. I damaged my back in a fall and soon the pain in my upper back became intolerable. Back in Manila and in the American hospital, I was told initially that I must be suffering either from a secondary carcinoma or else tuberculosis in my cervical spine. Later tests must have shown the doctors that I suffered from tuberculosis of the spine, for they told me I was to be put into a body cast for several months.

Then came grief. I wanted to go back. I wanted to be a part of the work that had grown precious to me and my colleagues and with tribal people who had grown dear to me. So I pleaded with the mission director and with the doctors to let me go back to Palawan in a cast. Foolishly, I thought it should be possible, but the refusal was firm. I wept, but my tears changed nothing.

Back to Boston

I gave no thought to supernatural healing, though curiously I had been healed of breast cancer that way without really realizing it. In Boston when I was twenty, one specialist told me after prolonged examination, blood tests, and X-rays, that a tumor in my left breast was malignant. It had been growing rapidly for several weeks and had been examined by more than one doctor. Immediate surgery was advised, but I was scared, confused, and hadn't wanted to make a decision.

The young people at Park Street Congregational Church prayed for me. So did a Pentecostal pastor in a church my aunt and I visited. Prayer was always good, but something of the simplicity of my childhood faith was lacking in that I never expected prayer to result in healing. Yet one day a little later I noticed that my breast was normal. I was hugely relieved. I would not have to go for an operation. Perhaps the doctors had been wrong. Perhaps it hadn't been cancer after all. The real significance of what had happened escaped me.

But about the healing of my spine there could be no doubt. I knew that other people had been praying for me, but when I was healed and on what I thought was my way back to the Philippines I met John White in a New Tribes boot camp; he told me of his strange experience in prayer for me, and I caught a glimpse of the mysterious ways in which God works through his people. What I did not immediately realize was that John was to play a bigger role in God's mysterious ways for me.

Off to Bolivia

In fact, the thought of marriage dismayed me. I wanted to go back to the work I loved. But God had other plans and to Bolivia John and I went.

Life became very full after that. There was another language to learn, another culture to absorb, new colleagues to get to know, new duties to fulfill—and motherhood. The fellowship in New Tribes was precious and real, and the work of enormous value. We were not always sure whether the work we were doing ourselves was all that significant, but there were some remarkable answers to prayer. We learned what it was to live by faith, and the supply of our needs was unquestionably miraculous.

John's ministry expanded, while mine progressively narrowed to the home and the children. After four years John assumed heavy responsibilities in university evangelism throughout Latin America and was loaned by the mission to the International Fellowship of Evangelical Students. We moved to Argentina to set up the Latin American office, and later on we went to Lima, Peru. Our five children were born in different Latin American countries.

They were curious years—tough (extremely so) and productive—yet often we felt we were beating the air. God worked, but something was wrong. John was away a lot. His responsibilities included the coordination of work in twenty-one countries, but shortage of funds meant that in one trip he would have to cover as many as seven or eight countries. But it wasn't that that troubled us, for God was working, students were being converted, and groups were being formed. National movements were beginning, leaders were emerging, and a literature program was born.

Always we had a sense that there was something we didn't know. From our first meeting the two of us had discussed it. Did conservative evangelicals really understand the nature of the Holy Spirit's power? Had the movement become defensive, reactionary? Had the conservative reaction to the Pentecostal errors also cut the movement off from something God wished to impart? We could not accept that the New Testament dealt with another age that had passed away for good. And we both sensed our powerlessness, even though we had real dealings with God in prayer. Moreover we felt like square pegs in round holes in Christian work.

Canada

I never resented "being stuck with the children." They were a ministry in themselves. But the assaults of the powers of darkness were many and furious, and eventually John's health broke down. In 1964 we returned to Canada after ten years of missionary work. Soon after returning home, John (who was a trained physician but who had been away from medicine for some years) took four years of psychiatric training.

Our lives became a little more ordered and organized but my own spiritual life was going downhill. The church in Winnipeg that had supported us on the mission field and had shown us much kindness, eventually rejected us. When they gave us a very lengthy doctrinal statement to sign, honesty compelled us to say that we didn't understand eschatology well enough to say whether Scripture taught a premillennial, pretribulation rapture or not. Moreover, John, while firmly believing in God's grace and sovereignty, could not be sure what Hebrews 6 meant.

The problems seem laughable now, but at that time it meant that we could not remain members of the church. We pleaded; we would not teach or discuss our doubts with anyone. All we wanted was fellowship, discipline, and a bit of normal church life while we recovered. But it would be too dangerous. We were "powerful people." Our "influence" would be inevitable. The church leaders were kind but very firm—we were not wanted. In some ways I think it hurt them as much as it did us. We could bring our children with us to the Sunday morning service—but that was all.

We retired to lick our wounds. Mine, I think, went even deeper than John's. Was this the end of our pursuit of God? Of our years of serving and seeking him? I grew angry and bitter. John dragged us around to other churches, but the deadness of those Sunday morning services appalled me. I saw and heard nothing of what had originally drawn me to Christ. The warmth of some of our mission field fellowship was entirely lacking.

I quit going with John. Even when one day he discovered a group meeting in a community club at the end of our street, he could not persuade me to go. They were a sort of Adullam's Cave group: rejects thrown out of another church. They invited John to preach to them, a reject preaching to rejects. What next?

Curiosity

One Sunday curiosity got the better of me and on a bitterly cold day I tried to find them. But the door of the building seemed to be locked. Snow was piled against it. Somehow the door symbolized both the rejection, the coldness, and the deadness I felt toward me and all around me.

I found the group at last and, a little reluctantly, I began to attend their meetings with the children. We decided to be a tiny church— about fifteen of us. Yet from that group there sprang a church whose influence and impact was for a time felt in all the city. It grew—rapidly. We bought a little building, which soon became too small, and began to build another next door. It was exciting. Hope was born again in us. Home groups were formed. But potential division was soon to rear its head.

One home group, the group that grew the most rapidly, was charismatic. The old guard, the original fifteen, regarded them with misgiving. John declared that our unity, whether we were charismatic or not, must be in Christ. If we were Christians then we must stick together.

From time to time I attended meetings of the charismatic group. Hippies and druggies and singles were being helped and healed. There was something powerfully attractive about the whole thing. I liked the songs they sang, particularly the psalms. Were the tongues, the prophecies, the "words of knowledge" really from God? I hoped they were. It would be so wonderful, but I could not be sure.

Other things in the group troubled me. There were dishonesties, even plain lies. Among some members of the group there seemed to be an unspoken commitment to "capture" the whole church to their way of thinking, a sense of intrigue. The older members of the church resented it.

In the end the charismatic group pulled out amicably enough on the surface, but afterwards ugly developments ensued. The prophecies became manipulative power plays, some of them positively evil. Some "words from the Lord" predicted the splitting of marriages in the group, and eventually one section of the group slipped into Ontario in the night, in response to a prophecy of a great new ministry. The "prophets" had done evil work, with disastrous results. Marriages were indeed split, and the prophets' own marriages were included.

There was no great new ministry—only sin and broken marriages. The wounds have taken years to heal and many are still not healed. The flame of my hope burned low. Was this what happened when you got baptized in the Spirit? The break-up hurt me deeply, and not only because I loved the people concerned. I had caught a glimpse of something I yearned for. But there was no middle ground, and the "package" as a whole was unacceptable.

Failing Health

Years passed. Our children grew up and the nest emptied. My husband became an internationally recognized writer, and the demands for us to speak at conferences and universities grew. By then he had for years taught psychiatry as a member of the faculty of a university. But after prayer we decided he should quit psychiatry and devote his remaining years to writing and preaching. We moved into the country and lived in a condominium beside a beautiful Canadian lake.

Beautiful? Well, yes and no. My health had deteriorated. First came coronary spasms and the need to have nitroglycerine tablets handy constantly. Then came a chest condition that had me coughing through the night. Medical investigations could not pin the thing down. John never complained, but I woke him repeatedly each night with my coughing. And though he was busy during the day, suddenly I found myself with nothing to do. Was this all there was to life? To be an invalid wife? I battled with resentment.

The doctors suspected I had bronchiectasis and the condition worsened. An accident in a lake had us clinging for an hour or so in icy water to an overturned sailboat. My chest deteriorated sharply. Plans were made for yet more chest X-rays, this time with a radioactive dye. But the radiographs were never taken.

I had begun to pray that God would let us become more active in the kingdom—more directly involved. Then came a telephone call from Ken Blue giving us his impressions of John Wimber. Was there some way in which we might know true spiritual authority and power in Christian work? We decided to visit Fuller and investigate for ourselves. I was excited, but cautious. What if it turned out to be the same as with the charismatic group in our church—another fiasco? Nevertheless, X-rays would have to wait.

Back Off, Or Else . . .

Fuller became a roller coaster experience. There were days when my heart sang. John Wimber's approach seemed so sane, so balanced. I saw real authority, real power, but none of the immaturity I had seen in the charismatic group in Winnipeg.

Wimber was not obsessed with phenomena but with obedience to Christ. In my private devotionals, the Gospels became alive in a way they had never done before. I was fifty-five years old, a former missionary and a conference speaker, yet for the first time I saw the compassion of Jesus and his interactions with the people. I saw the significance of it all in vivid colors for the first time.

But there were also days of fear and pain. Our children seemed to be paying for my new joy. One was injured in a car accident, another was rushed into the hospital with a bleeding ulcer, a third was unemployed and sick, a fourth had serious marital difficulties, and our oldest boy's wife was gravely ill with hepatitis in Mexico. The five blows came one after another, all during our time at Fuller.

We knew what it was about; by this time we were familiar with the pattern. We had discovered from years of experience that when John expounded certain passages of Scripture or when we pursued certain courses, trouble always followed. Always there was an ominous sense of "Back off, or else . . ." The warnings were not from God. It was scary, and we grieved over our children, but we decided not to back off.

But there were other griefs. At night I would sometimes weep as I thought of what we might have done on the mission field had we known then what we now knew. I had not realized it at the time, but I had not been adequately prepared for missionary work. I wept as I thought of missionaries struggling in primitive areas and darkened cities lacking the equipment for the warfare waged against them. True, I rejoiced over the Third World pastors and those missionaries who were members of the class. But I spent more time weeping before the Lord.

Regrets had to be laid aside. Instead we began to put into practice principles we now saw clearly. Sometimes people were healed; sometimes they weren't. But always they seemed to receive something good, if only new hope and quickened joy. I began to wonder about my chest and my heart. Perhaps they could be healed while we were about it. And one day I had a curious experience. As I was looking at Steve, one of John Wimber's helpers, it was as though a voice said, "That man will lay his hands on you and heal you."

Intimacy with God

And so it turned out. One Sunday night after a service in the Vineyard Church in Anaheim, I heard John Wimber announce that someone present had had "a bronchial condition for an extended period of time" and that the person had "serious difficulty sleeping and could not breathe deeply without coughing." My heart began to beat.

I went to the area he directed to receive prayer. And then I saw Steve.

At first he walked past me, then turned and stared at me. "Do you want prayer?" Did I want prayer! As Steve prayed I felt something like a golf ball collect in my throat. It was the weirdest sensation. Suddenly it jiggled its way downwards like a ball in a slot machine and clunked on my diaphragm (at least that's what it felt like). Then it was gone. I took deep breaths and found my cough was gone, too. I was healed! That night we slept through the night for the first time in over two years.

A week or so later Steve prayed for me again—and since that time (now more than three years ago) I have needed no nitroglycerine and have no chest pain. Always a person with "a weak chest," I now have occasional colds like anyone else—but no bronchitis afterwards.

Grateful as I was for my own healing, I was even more grateful to find what I had been looking for all my life, a great degree of intimacy with the Lord and an entrance into the world of the New Testament. It wasn't that I had arrived; in fact, I had scarcely begun. But I now had the sense of knowing where I was going. I was a train that had found the tracks I was designed for.

On the Road Again

We sold our condominium. John had nearly three years of meetings and conferences lined up in Asia, Australia, and Latin America, so we began to live out of a suitcase. But for me there has been a new and growing excitement. We were more genuinely partners in the work, ministering side by side. We hated the unending travel, but we exulted in seeing Christ's victories and authority. Having felt the tug of compassion, it was so good to be able to help people more effectively—physically, emotionally, spiritually. Compassion without the power to help can be depressing and painful.

I cannot pretend it is unadulterated glory. Life still has ups and downs, joys and sorrows. But we feel ten years younger, and there is an excitement and purpose to our lives that the years had stolen away. We thought we believed the Scriptures were true. We see now that we had unwittingly cut portions of them out just the same way liberal scholars do. (Fundamentalists have their own ways of theologizing away the authority of Scripture. What is the point of protesting its inerrancy while solemnly saying certain Scriptures "don't apply to us now"?) And what's the point of any of our protestations when we don't act on Scripture?

Scripture is true, and I'm running the risk (which is no risk at all) of counting on it. My appetite for this new life is voracious. A feast is ahead of me—an enormous feast. So far I'm only nibbling the hors d'oeuvres.

15

Fully Anglican, Fully Renewed

David Pytches

Bishop David Pytches is vicar of St. Andrew's Anglican Church in Chorleywood, Hertfordshire, England. He has served as a missionary in Latin America. He and his wife, Mary, have four children.

John Wimber and a team from Orange County came to St. Andrew's Church, Chorleywood, in 1981. John comments on this visit in his book *Power Evangelism*. Suffice it to say that neither the church nor our ministry has been the same since—and that's putting it mildly. The changes have been powerful and dramatic.

So that you may appreciate the significance of the changes, I need to explain my background. I was brought up in a Suffolk village—the ninth child (sixth son out of seven) in a family of ten. My father was the rector of the parish. My early education was with a governess to the family, who also taught two other children from the village. After that it was away to boarding schools, army, university, and theological college. Ours was a very happy and secure home and during the holidays there were always enough of us to be able to make up opposing teams for all the games kids love to play.

My parents' solid goodness and faith so impressed itself upon me that I was feeling a call to serve the Lord before I even had the assurance of being "saved." This came to me when as a child of about five there was a tent mission to village children in the parish. The evangelist spelled out the gospel in very simple terms and I first felt joy in the assurance that I was already a child of God through faith in Jesus Christ. From then on there was never really anything but to press on till I was ordained as a minister in the Church of England. People used to smile and say "so you are following in your father's foot-steps," which used to confuse me because that was not the reason I was doing it, though in one sense I was following in his footsteps. My father had had an interesting spiritual pilgrimage in that he was actu-ally converted after ordination. My mother's father had also been or-dained, as had my direct forbears for seven generations back bar one. Both my youngest and oldest brothers followed into the ordained ministry, as did a medical brother-in-law. My son-in-law is to be or-dained shortly. You could say we have ordination in the blood!

Chol Chol, Chile

I served my first curacy in St. Ebbe's Church in Oxford, where I met the girl who was to be my wife—Mary Trevisick, whose questing spirit for the things of God has continually challenged and inspired me during nearly thirty years of marriage. She was then secretary of the Young People's Fellowship at St. Ebbe's, where she had been converted. After three years at Oxford Mary and I moved to St. Pat-rick's, Wallington, where we just had time to have our first baby, Charlotte, before the door opened to the mission field. We had tried this door, believing that as disciples we should be willing to go any-where for Jesus. We secretly hoped that it was not God's will. We felt ourselves unworthy and feared we would make a hash of the new lan-guage required for the work. After ten years in Chile they told us we spoke Spanish like natives—of England!

By October 1959 we were on our way to South America, where to begin with we worked where others had labored amongst the Arau-canian Indians. Our base was Chol Chol, some twenty miles from Temuco in central Chile. Access to most of the churches, many of them tucked away in the foothills of the Andes, was on horseback. The very real faith of these Araucanians confirmed for me the relevance of the gospel in a completely different culture. I questioned some of them about their love for Jesus. They explained that when the first missionaries came to share the gospel they found that through the name of Jesus the spirits of darkness and fear were driven back. These animists were being set free. Such spiritual power in the name of Jesus was new to me. I thought God had sent me to Chile to teach. I soon discovered that he had sent me there to learn. I hope I am still learning!

My Anglican traditions died hard. I remember riding out to these churches with ecclesiastical robes in my saddlebags. On arrival I would seek out a suitable mimosa tree, behind which I could decently attire myself before entering a hut of a church building. Not only was it difficult to reconcile my traditions with this culture, it was also difficult to reconcile myself with my transport. My horse and I never really got on too well together. The horse's name was "Bomba Atomica!"

Goodbye to Bomba

When a call came to go to Valparaiso in 1962 I accepted with alacrity. It was a happy goodbye to "Bomba Atomica" and all that. Valparaiso was the biggest port on the west coast of South America. Our mandate was to plant churches in that urban environment. We started in an old English church building on one of the hills overlooking the harbor. Two or three years later we founded our first daughter church almost by accident. One member of the congregation, Senora Fresia, had moved about ten miles away to a new housing estate the other side of Vina del Mar, a seaside resort and twin city with Valparaiso. She had asked us to her house for a meal. After we had eaten, Fresia said, "Wouldn't it be nice to have a church here in Gomez Carreno? There are forty thousand people here on this estate with nowhere to worship."

"Yes," I said, "but wherever could we have it?"

"Why here," she said with an arm flourish around her little front room. I nearly turned the idea down flat, thinking a church organ would not fit there! In the days before I left England we had never thought of singing hymns in a church service without a wind organ. But the Lord seemed to be telling me that this was the place to start, so we did. It was then I remembered visiting the site some two years before and praying that God would raise up a church there to his glory! But I never thought it would begin like that.

Over the years God blessed us and we saw other churches added. We were having to take great liberties with Anglicanism. If we were to encourage the spontaneous expansion of the church and have new congregations be self-supporting and self-governing, then the Chilean converts had to be encouraged to do things their way. This did not seem to be approved of by our church superiors and by 1969, feeling very misunderstood, we argued that ten years had been a fair crack-of-the-whip and we were now ready to settle back in the United Kingdom. The Lord clearly had other plans, however, and told us in a remarkable way to go back to Chile at the end of that year.

My wife remembers walking up the gangway of the S.S. Pasteur with our four girls, muttering, "Lord, you will simply have to do something for me on this voyage. I can't get off this ship the way I am getting on." Well, the Lord is always full of surprises. Something good seemed to have happened to a missionary who was traveling with us. She had somehow been renewed by the Holy Spirit. Mary was suspicious and spent a long time arguing with her. "All right," she said, "tell me really what it did for you?" And the missionary replied, "It was just like falling in love with Jesus." "That's precisely what I want," thought Mary. And like the wrestling Jacob, she would not now let him go till the Spirit of God had touched her life in renewal.

Two down, one to go! That was me. I was ready to argue; I knew how dangerous all this stuff could be. I had a very sound orthodox evangelical upbringing. But I found a new and beautiful dimension had been brought into our marriage and six months later I was asking for such an anointing too. By that stage I had become a bishop. After a lot of repenting I came to know the blessing of renewal in my own life. I now believed the gifts of the Spirit to be authentic for today, but I pastored a church in which I was prevented from working out the implications of this ministry. We went through an earthquake and a revolution and saw God doing marvelous things. Many were coming to the Lord, but we still had little idea of how to integrate the gifts into the life of the churches. It was bewildering indeed.

Back to Britain

Then in 1976 we took our two youngest girls to join their sisters at school in the United Kingdom. For a variety of reasons it suddenly became clear that all the girls really needed their parents nearby and we resigned (January 1, 1977) with nowhere to go. Around March, Dr. Robert Runcie, then Bishop of St. Albans, asked me to consider a call to take over the leadership of St. Andrew's, Chorleywood. This was an exciting challenge. The congregation had been lovingly built up by my predecessors, John and Gay Perry. Several church members had come into renewal under their ministry. A friend said I would be a fool to take on the job, as there was only one way that church could go—down! But we felt convinced that it was God's call, which he confirmed to us in a remarkable way, and I accepted the appointment. I was looking forward to learning more about ministering in the gifts of the Spirit. There had been a lot of teaching on the Holy Spirit at St. Andrew's, but in my ignorance of how to coordinate renewal I soon began to feel that something good was slipping out of our grasp.

A former missionary friend, Eddie Gibbs, had moved to Chorleywood and he was studying "church growth" for a further degree. His research took him to California, where he visited a number of churches experiencing growth. One impressed him particularly. It was called the "Vineyard Christian Fellowship." Dr. Gibbs wrote to the late Canon David Watson, who used to lecture each year at Fuller Seminary, and urged him to go and see this church. David Watson discovered a kindred spirit in the pastor of the Vineyard, John Wimber, and a firm friendship developed. David told Eddie that after his visit to Vineyard his ministry would never be the same again. This was impressive indeed. What David did today we all tried to do to-morrow. I learned that David was inviting John Wimber to the United Kingdom, so I wrote at once and urged John to come to St. Andrew's on his way to York, as we were so conveniently near to Heathrow Airport, London.

Early in 1981 John replied that he would come. He arrived for the weekend of Pentecost with a team of nearly thirty. I could not imagine at that stage whatever he wanted all that lot for. We were soon to see. It was a memorable weekend. I had never seen a person's sight restored before—that was just one miracle among many. But more than that, there were conversions, people were renewed and anointed—some were laid out on the floor in the power of the Holy Spirit. The place was electric. Everything was happening. The whole of John's team were praying for our people everywhere all over the building.

On the last evening some eighteen to twenty people were anointed with a gift for healing. This was an embarrassment indeed! Whatever were we going to do with them all? How could we integrate these gifts into the life of the church? We had a very respectable "Folk Communion" once a month on one Sunday evening where we prayed for the sick, although we never saw much fruit from this heal-ing ministry. It was all nice and Anglican. The clergy prayed from the sanctuary side and the lay helpers approached from behind the sick people who were kneeling. How could we fit any more into this? We were already ministering six to one!

So we did the only thing we could. We arranged to meet early each day to pray. At the end of the week we met to discuss what the Lord might be saying to us. We felt quite clearly that he wanted us to begin ministering healing after every major service in church. Whenever the Word was preached we would expect the Lord to confirm it with signs following (Mark 16).

American Visit

When John and Carol Wimber were leaving, they suggested we come visit them in California. We put this down to American charm and politeness, never thinking they really meant it. When John and Carol returned to England the following year we learned that they were really disappointed that we had not taken up their kind offer. So we booked flight tickets immediately and went. We were able to see the Vineyard Christian Fellowship functioning at close hand and we were overwhelmed by the worship—it was so beautiful and tender, so God-focused. We felt our hearts melt toward him. And at last we saw a model of a church that incorporated the gifts of the Spirit so wholesomely in worship. Between worshiping God and ministering to those in need there was the ministry of the Word with John Wimber expounding from one of the Letters in his inimitable way. It was laid-back and low-key. We found it all so appealing.

After the service had ended a huge number stayed for more ministry. Mary and I watched an elderly black woman shuffle up on her walker, obviously with very bad leg problems. A couple from the Vineyard took her to one side to pray. We were told we could join ourselves to any couples praying for the sick, but that one looked like a hard one, so we linked up with a couple who were praying for a man with a bad headache—we had thought it would be good to start with something easy. Imagine both our delight and disappointment when we heard a shout behind us. The old woman was striding out of the building, stamping her feet and shouting, "Praise you, Jesus!" Her husband was rushing along behind her, bearing the discarded zimmer. We had missed it! We could have been with that couple and seen the woman healed under our very eyes.

That night I joined myself to a group of three young people who were praying for a middle-aged woman. She couldn't see out of one eye. These young people prayed and waited and waited and waited. "They don't know what on earth to do," I thought. I began looking around for others still ministering to take myself where something was happening. But I then thought, "These young people have great patience and they do not look at all embarrassed or agitated. If they can wait, so can I." After about twenty minutes the lady we were praying for suddenly embraced the most vocal of the group and cried excitedly, "I can see! I can see! To God be the glory!" The more we saw the more we liked. Here was a Christian fellowship where they preached Christ, believed the Word, and ministered in power. They were in no way bound by any set of rules, simply bonded by an accepted range of biblical values.

Lord of the Church

One of these was that the Holy Spirit should be the administrator of the church. This sounded strange to a good Anglican like me who had trained himself for over twenty-five years in the ordained ministry of the church to be two steps ahead of the Holy Spirit. After all, one could not be sure that the Holy Spirit would always follow the instructions for conducting our Prayer Book rituals! Had anything untoward ever happened during a time a worship, such as a church member being overwhelmed by the Holy Spirit (which was highly unlikely in any case), I would have announced a hymn for the congregation to sing while beckoning to the wardens to carry out the offending body to the vestry and to sit on him until the men in white coats arrived.

But we were being reminded of something I had heard before, but had never really thought much about—that the Son of God only did what he saw the Father doing (John 5:19). John Wimber shared with us how the Lord had spoken to him once and said, "John, I've seen your ministry. Now I want to show you mine." Jesus only did what he saw the Father doing—we needed to begin learning to do the same. One way for this was through the revelatory gifts of the Spirit, discernment, words of knowledge, and of wisdom (1 Cor. 12).

Soon we were learning how to operate in these gifts that God distributes sovereignly to his church when it is gathered to worship him. This was a completely new ball game. During the previous years of my ordained ministry I had been accustomed to making my own plans for the church and asking God to bless them. Now we were learning to discern what God was doing and then to bless that. It was amazing to discover how glorifying to God that kind of ministry could be. This was a vital link we had missed when we started ministering in the power of the Holy Spirit at St. Andrew's immediately following John's first visit. We had teams praying for the sick, but we had not seen how important it was to be discerning what God was doing and then to bless and honor that. We had not discovered how "words of knowledge"—fragments of divine insight—could show us *what* to pray for and "words of wisdom" (among other things) teach us *how* and *when* to pray.

Obviously the church would need regular teaching. There was no corpus of wisdom on ministering in the power of the Spirit from within our own tradition. I asked John why he had not written a book about it. He said he had not had time and suggested I have a go. By borrowing notes from John, by regular teaching, and by growing in personal experience through ministering in the power of the Holy Spirit I put some material together. So as not to exalt one local church, I sought also to gather insights and illustrations from other Christian traditions—especially the case of the Englishman Smith Wigglesworth, a one-time Bradford plumber, who had been used by God to raise fourteen people from the dead. I had never heard of this mighty servant of God before. He had died the year before I entered theological college and I was not to hear of him for another twenty-five years. Wigglesworth exercised an extraordinarily powerful ministry worldwide to the glory of God for over fifty years. Here had been a humble and holy man who, because he was not of our tradition, had been completely ignored by those training us to minister.

My book *Come Holy Spirit,* published by Hodder and Stoughton, appeared eventually in 1985. This was designed to give practical help to those learning to minister in power, especially those in our own church. Meanwhile we encouraged other churches who wanted to get started to send teams to join us in our teach-ins using the material from *Come Holy Spirit.* We also started a monthly week-night celebration, where church leaders could send their members to get saved, empowered, renewed, anointed, or whatever God wanted to do for them. The celebrations, like the teach-ins, have had amazing attendances and blessings.

Faith Sharing Teams

For some years our church had been sending out "Faith Sharing Teams" under the leadership of the Reverend Barry Kissell (this is described in his book *Springtime in the Church*). The objective was to encourage lay people to share their faith and so evangelize. These teams went out with their testimonies and a dance and drama group for good measure. Now the emphasis has changed. As the teams have begun to minister in power, God has begun to supply the dance and drama!

Invitations to other churches increased considerably and there was a time when there have been up to five teams away ministering in other churches during a given weekend. The lovely thing is that there seems to be no denominational barriers. Invitations come from the whole spectrum of the Christian church and from all over the world. We are not able to respond ourselves to all of them and pass on many to other churches who are developing a similar kind of ministry. Barry Kissell has recorded his wide experience in this ministry in his latest book, *Walking on Water*.

When John first visited us, I was worried about how we could possibly contribute significantly to his and his teams' expenses. He refused our poor offering. "No," he said, "this is our church's mission. We ask nothing of you for ourselves—only remember what Jesus taught when he said, 'freely you have received, freely give.' " If we had received anything through that visit we were to give it away. Apart from Faith Sharing, one way we could do this was in helping to train other churches. Some were having real difficulties in getting going. It seemed important to bring these leaders together. Without wanting to control these brethren in any way, we felt the need to do what we could to enable leaders in various parts of the country to get together and encourage each other to press on in a ministry of Holy Spirit power. We invited the leaders of these small groups to meet together from time to time to share reports and ideas.

It seemed right also to arrange a leaders' day once or twice a year, where we could give a little teaching, share experiences in starting the ministry in the local church, and provide ministry to the many leaders who have never been ministered to before in this way. We did not publish the precise subject matter or the speakers invited for these leaders' days. We simply circulated the times and dates to the clergy and other church leaders on our mailing list. The days were so well attended—between four and five hundred present—that we then decided to have two separate days to make room for double the number. Again the church filled up. We now have three days, all full. These clergy and pastors come from all denominations, bringing some of their local church leaders with them. A similar day conference is regularly held in the north of England at Sheffield led by Canon Robert Warren. They too have split into two days and are having problems with large numbers.

Anglican

Some people have asked if one can adopt the values of the Vineyard and remain with a traditional church. The answer is yes, one can adopt most of them. We are encouraged in St. Andrew's. That is not to say we have not had many problems and still have a very long way to go. We certainly need to better our pulpit ministry in the teaching of the Word of God and develop our church home groups. We cannot easily experiment with church planting, due to the Anglican parish system, but we are free to go out and share life with other churches. We have real support and encouragement from the diocesan authorities, who may not necessarily identify with all that we are doing. We have also noted that the largest number of church leaders at the Wimber conferences come from Anglican churches; many of these are now trying to get things going in their local parishes. We want to help them in every way we can. Besides regular teach-ins for local churches, we are doing this quite frequently in residential conferences across Britain and beyond.

A further development has been the ministry of binding up the brokenhearted, often called inner healing. My wife, Mary, has been closely involved with the development of this ministry in the local church and has put down guiding principles, together with some practical experiences, in her new book *Set My People Free*.

It will come as no surprise to record that after our initial experience with the Vineyard the worship for the church here has changed. The ministry of the church has developed, diversified, and multiplied. Our leadership roles have been revolutionized. Though we have had and still have many failures, we look forward to the future with new hope and joyful anticipation. Wherever the Holy Spirit is welcomed there we see the Lord Jesus Christ being glorified.

16

Chased by the Dragon

Jackie Pullinger

In 1966 Jackie Pullinger left her native England for the Far East, eventually landing in Hong Kong. Since that time she has worked as a missionary in the giant slum called the Walled City. In her book Chasing the Dragon *she tells of how she ministered there; here she updates her story.*

God told me to go to the mission field long before I became a Christian. With awful certainty I knew that God got you in the end, and so I concluded that it would be smarter to be on his side from the beginning. I was five when I worked that out, but not until studying for a music degree at the Royal College in London many years later did I understand that Jesus had died to bring me into relationship with his Father and that I needed to appropriate that.

"Funny," I thought, "why didn't anyone tell me before that I've been living off a presumptuous relationship?" After all, in my heart I'd been saying the "Our Father" prayer for thirteen years. Anyway, I thanked Jesus for dying for me and began what I now think of as the unfair Christian life. I knew I was going to heaven; I was filled with joy unspeakable and immediately wanted to share this with those who hadn't heard of God's extraordinary love.

I suppose some people would say I'd been converted at that moment, but as I looked back over the years I could see that God had planted in me a heart for him long before that. It was receiving salvation for myself that brought assurance of sins forgiven and the knowledge that I could actually enjoy what Jesus had laid hold of for me. The more I learned of what Jesus had made available for me the more I enjoyed it as I appropriated it.

My relationship with the Holy Spirit has been similar. In retrospect I see him working a desire for his fellowship in me and even causing me to experience signs and miracles long before I understood the power available. Appropriating the power later was important, but even more important was learning how to walk in it.

The year 1966 was the start of the Cultural Revolution in mainland China and I arrived in Hong Kong in November quite flushed with faith. I was longing to share God's love with the people. I *knew* God had led me there. I'd had a dream, vision, and prophecy all directing me to "Go!"

"Very irresponsible," said a missionary society when they heard that my Anglican minister had told me to get onto a ship calling in as many different ports as possible and pray to know where to get off. But I knew God had been speaking, although at that time I didn't understand this was the spiritual gift of a word of wisdom. When I'd left England in 1966 no one talked about the Holy Spirit or his gifts, though we did mention the Holy Ghost in the creed and at Confirmation.

"It's Very Dangerous"

It was soon all too obvious that I needed to find out about power from God's Spirit, however, for he led me to a city of utmost horror and depravity. The Walled City within Kowloon was the name for a giant slum of nearly sixty thousand people crammed into six acres of land. There was no official water or electricity supply; stinking open sewers lined the dark narrow alleys. Gangs similar to the Mafia ruled the area's brothels and drug and gambling dens.

The condition of the people was appalling; I knew many were sick and dying both spiritually and physically. At one time the bodies of addicts who had died in the night were piled beside the Walled City's only toilet for collection in the morning. Simply mouthing words like "Jesus loves you" no longer seemed appropriate when trying to show these heroin addicts, gangsters, diseased street sleepers, and sixty-year-old prostitutes the heart of God they'd never heard of. I wanted something real, and I saw that if I believed the Bible as I'd been taught, I should be able to heal the sick instead of handing them tracts and see addicts delivered instead of merely referring them to clinics. I wanted to do as Jesus did.

I dreamed of walking into heroin dens, laying hands on people, and seeing them saved. I dreamed of praying with the blind in the dark lanes, touching them, and watching their eyes open. As I saw homeless twelve-year-old boys being used by the gangs as pimps and drug pushers I said, "God, it would be worth my whole life if you would use me to save just one."

"Be careful—it's very dangerous," I was told as I searched for the Holy Spirit in action. But I could see that that wasn't true; the Bible said the Holy Spirit was of peace, not fear and division. I visited Pentecostal churches in the hope of finding some answers and vaguely remembered my mother telling me the people rolled in the aisles. No such things in Hong Kong, though; only some loud wailing and clapping and shouting—no power, no gifts of the Spirit. By this time I'd read up on the gifts and was longing to see them in action.

My search proved fruitless, however, and I concluded that this stuff was only for advanced Christians, as I'd heard that my two spiritual mentors in England, David Watson and David MacInnes, Anglican ministers, had miraculous gifts. I was told they had the gift of tongues and gift of healing. But I was also told that one must not discuss it. Finally I collared some Pentecostal missionaries who told me that in Hong Kong their society had made a pact with the conservative evangelicals not to talk about the Holy Spirit, because they were to be united in Jesus. This did not seem to help the hundreds of people I saw perishing around me, so I went on praying.

Nothing Happened

"They've got it!" I thought. I knew I'd found it when I met a young Chinese couple near the Walled City who shone with God's presence. But judging from our first words, you wouldn't have known it. We had quite an argument.

"You haven't got the Holy Spirit," they said.

"Oh yes I have," I replied, confident I was right because I'd asked for the Spirit and knew you got what you asked for.

"No you haven't," they continued.

"Oh yes I have," I countered. I *was* right; how else could I believe in Jesus if I didn't have the Spirit? I *knew* I was right. We went on arguing. I knew I was right. Actually I *was* right. But the fact remained that I could see that this couple had something I didn't and I realized that all I was arguing about was semantics. Whether it was "the baptism of the Holy Spirit," "the outpouring of," "the gift of," "the infilling of," "the fullness of," "the power of" I no longer cared. "Dear Lord," I prayed silently. "If you have anything from your Spirit that will help me to make you *real* to people, please give it to me—and I'll decide what to call it later."

So I visited this couple's home and they laid hands on me and prayed, telling me to open my mouth and I would speak in a new language. Of course I longed for this gift—I thought it would be wonderful to be able to pray all the things I couldn't express in my own words. I just wasn't going to do it when *they* told me. God would do it, wouldn't he, if he wanted me to have it? I kept my mouth shut. Nothing happened.

Finally, because I was hot, sticking to the chair, and feeling sorry for the couple because they had expected me to perform, I opened my mouth to ask God's help and immediately began speaking in a new language. I knew it was from God. My oboe tonguing technique had never been good; for my tongue to have moved so fast had to be God's doing.

My only emotion that day was embarrassment. "Thank God," I said, "that they weren't British." And then I ran for the door while the poor couple were trying to tell me that now I could expect other gifts like healing, prophecy, discernment of spirits, and so on. "Thank you so much," I said and went home to wait. Nothing happened.

I tried praying in tongues but it didn't make me feel close to God.

It didn't make me feel anything, really. So I stopped. What a disappointment. I thought that this experience would change everything, but I seemed no nearer to Jesus. I wasn't healing the sick or leading people to Christ. I just worked and worked with everything I had day and night, hoping to show a dying and desperate people Christ's love. I gave them food, found them homes, and clothed them. They were impressed but not changed; they recognized Jesus but were not converted. "If only it were true," I thought, "that receiving the power of the Holy Spirit would change everything."

Rude to God

It was not until the following year, 1968, that I met an American couple who straightaway asked if I prayed in tongues. I replied that I didn't because I thought maybe I had received the wrong thing when I had prayed with the Chinese couple. Everyone else I had read about had felt wonderful—"bathed in love," "lifted up to a mountain," "floating on a cloud," and so on.

"You're very rude to God," said my friends. "Whatever made you mistake the gift of the Spirit for the gift of emotion? You're a good evangelical. The Bible says if you speak in tongues you will grow spiritually; it doesn't say you'll *feel* spiritual. You asked for power to preach the gospel. Now get on and use it!" And they made me.

By the clock I prayed fifteen minutes a day in the language of the Spirit and still felt nothing as I asked the Spirit to help me intercede for those he wanted to reach. After about six weeks of this I began to lead people to Jesus without trying. Gangsters fell to their knees sobbing in the streets, women were healed, heroin addicts were miraculously set free. And I knew it all had nothing to do with me.

It was a set-up. As I prayed in the Spirit, in a mysterious way God led me to the right person in the right place and at the right time. All I had to say were the words. And sometimes, irreverently, I had the impression that if I said "tomato ketchup" they would have been saved. They were so ready—whatever I said, they heard and saw Jesus. Then I was filled with emotion.

Receiving and using the power of the Spirit has been like that for me. Usually I have no feeling at all receiving and using gifts, but as I see them help others I am deeply moved.

With my friends I began to learn about the other gifts of the Spirit and we experienced a remarkable few years of ministry. Scores of gangsters and well-to-do people, students and churchpeople were converted and all received a new language to pray in private and other gifts to use when meeting together. We opened several homes to house heroin addicts and all were delivered from drugs painlessly because of the power of the Holy Spirit.

Creeping Pride

When visiting England and friends abroad I told of these miracles and found that people were curious about tongues. Because of fear about overemphasis of this "unimportant gift" it seemed that most churches, ministers, and renewal meetings had reacted by not mentioning tongues at all. I met hundreds of people who'd prayed for the power of the Spirit and who wondered if they had it. They hadn't spoken in tongues. Some had fallen over; some had experienced joy; and some had wept. But few had power to be witnesses, and they knew nothing of other spiritual gifts either.

With some testimony, teachings, and demonstration I found that God enabled me to lead them into actualizing the power of the Spirit and that all could then receive the gift of a new language for prayer. The annoying thing was that ministers began to say I had a special ministry in helping people receive the gift of tongues, whereas I knew that anyone could be used in this way if they were willing. I just had more practice than many people, because I practiced it more.

The years went by and our houses in Hong Kong grew. Our answer for nearly all problems was "pray in tongues," which seemed to work quite well. How exactly it happened I don't know, but pride and exclusiveness crept in. We began to despise other churches and fellowships that didn't know the freedom of the Spirit as we did. We taught that Christ was coming back for a pure bride and that a few holy Christians were better than hundreds of bad-living ones. We dismissed big churches out-of-hand, as they couldn't possibly know everything all their members were up to.

Our drive for "purity" meant people who fell back into sin were excluded from our fellowship. But this created a disastrous situation for the ministry: in the end I had nowhere to bring new converts. The very fellowship that had sprung up to nurture these despised, weak, poor, dying people excluded them because they might not be serious enough about Jesus, because they might contaminate others. I could not leave, so I asked God what I should do. I prayed, but I received no answer for a year.

No Place to Go

I knew I could not start another group, for that would split our church. Many of the Christians—and gangsters and prostitutes with amazing testimonies and healings—had fallen away from the group and, because they were not serious enough to "shape up," we were not allowed to look for them. The fellowship was shrinking and my future was unclear.

So during 1982 I decided to receive further training in teaching English as a second language. At least then, I thought, I could teach in mainland China and minister there. I had written a book about what God had done among us but it was embarrassing to talk about it, as this had all seemed to have been lost. No longer was it an adventure, no longer did we feel we would die for the people; no longer was it joyful. My American friends felt they were not called to addicts anymore. They felt my ministry in the Walled City was over. So what was I to do now?

The charismatic ministry interlude had been exciting, fruitful, and promising. But now it seemed we had done it, knew it all, and it had become damp and soggy. We had settled for another dispensation. The exciting power had happened to start us off, but now we had good teaching to keep us going. The test of a good meeting was to have tongues, interpretations, and prophecies, but we didn't seem to listen to what God said through them. Having the gifts, we thought, was enough.

"Wimberland"

Then my friend Nicole went to spend a week in California. She returned and told me of John Wimber's ministry and teaching on healing. I was not that impressed with what she said, because, after all, we prayed for the sick too and a few occasionally got well. But the more she told me the more I sensed a stirring in my spirit.

John Wimber taught on healing. He had models and demonstrations. Now, it seemed to me that if everyone we prayed with received the gift of tongues because we took the time to explain and teach them in a relaxed manner, then we could learn from others who were experienced in other areas of ministry like healing. At that time I didn't know about how sometimes God imparts ministry through one Christian to another, but I sensed that if we stuck around those who were doing it soon we too would do it. So early in 1983 I made plans to go to "Wimberland," as Nicole dubbed it.

Seven days before going a blow fell. My American co-workers had already returned to the United States over a year before, leaving a young husband and wife to pastor our group. This couple announced that they were leaving and wouldn't be coming back to our meeting. By the time I boarded the plane for California I knew that most of the fellowship, all the good people anyway, had followed them. I was confused and broken.

"How's the work, Jackie?" asked John that first evening in the United States.

"What work?" I muttered, and my eyes filled with tears as I wondered if there would be anyone at all left in our fellowship to return to ten days later.

"I'm sorry, but I know you only have a short time here and I want to help you," said John. (*How did he know?* I thought.)

That night several Vineyard leaders came together and I was invited to join them. Toward the end of the evening we prayed for each other. One by one as they were ministered to they began to cry, some of them deeply with racking sobs. *I'm not going to do that,* I thought. Even though until then my experience of the Spirit had been extremely powerful, it was without a show of emotions. But I did cry and my back felt warm as Bob Fulton laid his hand on it. I had an injured shoulder that was screaming with pain. "The Spirit keeps coming on you and then lifting off, then coming again," Bob said. I was unused to his terminology, but felt a warmth come in waves. They prayed for me with knowledge and words that had to have come from God. They were so personal, so probing. I was impressed. I couldn't have cared less about my crying or running mascara; I knew God was there.

After about thirty minutes John said, "She can't take any more; there's a curse over her. I can see it. It's a 'Christian curse' [a curse spoken by a Christian]. It's words spoken over her that are not true. I can see it like a tight band over her forehead."

As soon as he said it I knew what he meant, though it didn't square with what I'd been taught—that Christians couldn't be troubled by demons, let alone curses.

Further Prayer

John suggested I receive further prayer that week for my shoulder and so I went to every meeting I could. I must have received about thirty hours of prayer, learning much about praying for the sick and inner healing as I was prayed for myself.

"How are you *feeling?*" This seemed an intrusion. When I was being prayed for I didn't feel like talking to people, but they kept on asking questions like "What's God doing?" Eventually I decided to be a good sport and answer them—they tried so hard. So I learned the value of communicating and cooperating with what the Spirit was doing. I began to understand what John meant when he talked about "doing what the Father is doing."

I received prayer both from healing experts and from learners and beginners. They prayed in different ways but they all loved me and never grew weary of praying. I learned to receive ministry, was encouraged to forgive where I'd been hurt, and cried most of the time. And I gave up wearing eye makeup for the week.

By this time I was not worried about the demon teaching. I'd heard testimony and teaching, seen demonstration, and wondered why the sickness came because of Satan; it seemed that Christians were affected by both.

But each time I went to a meeting my pain became more acute until I was actually screaming loudly (I, who had been afraid to sob). When John heard about it he said it was time to fix it and so he and others prayed against the curse and broke it. My shoulder was healed and the pain ceased. "And never do that again," Bob instructed me quite angrily. "You were under bondage, but you allowed yourself to be. Never again give away your ministry."

I knew what I had been freed from and asked whether all my spiritual children in Hong Kong had to receive thirty hours of prayer before they too were freed. John told me that all those that were related to me spiritually had been freed as I had been, but I might have to apologize to a few of them.

Home Again

So I returned to Hong Kong to begin from scratch again. Over the next few months the remaining members of the fellowship left but new converts arrived. We taught on healing, inviting the Holy Spirit to come and minister in our gatherings. Our meetings were not as predictable as they had been before I went to California, and slowly we began to grow in our understanding and experience of worship and our love for God and each other.

During that year nearly all those who had fallen away from our group over the past decade came back. This included addicts who had left our houses and returned to drugs. They didn't all stay but they knew they were welcome and that there was a place of mercy and forgiveness. I was amazed and overwhelmed with gladness. I never had to look for any of them. Even though we'd changed addresses several times the Lord caused the ones we'd lost to find us or to run into us on the streets. I apologized to a few and they understood. Once again my home filled up with those wanting to quit drugs and find new life in Christ.

During the next two years we rented more and more apartments to house those who found hope in Christ's love. Many were delivered from heroin and stayed on to help look after the growing number who sought healing. As most had been homeless or were living in drug dens before that, they had no place of their own to return to. I didn't believe that the kingdom of God would be limited only to a few each year, but we had no more room in our apartments. So we prayed that the Lord would multiply our resources in every way.

It was as if heaven opened up. We were offered an old temporary resettlement area in Kowloon. Without our even applying for it the Hong Kong government gave us a large area with fourteen long tin huts where we could accommodate all the recovered addicts, teach them work skills, and prepare them as ministers. We've taken in battered wives, street sleepers, and abused children. One old ex-prostitute who lives with us had been selling herself for fifty years before she came to believe in Jesus at the age of sixty-seven. The people who owned her were injecting her three times a day with heroin in her back because she had used up all the veins in her arms and legs. She was set free from heroin as the Holy Spirit came on her and she had a pain-free withdrawal.

We see the sick healed, demons cast out, and the hungry fed regularly. Wives are reconciled with their husbands and whole families converted. We've opened our own T-shirt factory, a barber shop, and a garment sewing shop. The fellowship is rapidly growing, numbering several hundred on Sunday; local pastors slip in to find out why we are growing at a rate phenomenal for Hong Kong. People from the highest social classes are touched and become Christians as they see the lowest in the land transformed by Jesus. Some just walk into our camp and believe in Jesus without our having to speak a word. "I felt the love of God as soon as I walked into your place," we've heard them say. "It was so amazing . . . I didn't want to leave."

Lau Leung in his sixties had sixty-seven previous criminal convictions and had slept in the streets for thirty years. He was emaciated, covered with lice, and slimy, and he was forced to commit robberies daily to feed his drug habit. His brother, who had a home and was a Christian, tried to lead him to Jesus by reading the Bible to him and couldn't understand why he didn't respond. When I heard about this I invited Lau Leung to the best teahouse I could find. He took one look at the man I brought with me and said, "Why is he so fat?" My man, an ex-policeman and ex-addict, replied, "Jesus did it!"

"Right," said Lau Leung, "I'll take Jesus," and he prayed to receive a new life right there at the table. It turned out that the two men had been in prison together before and Lau Leung knew that addicts like him can't get fat. They are too poor and too sick. The Holy Spirit filled him and he began to lead a new life. He and another old man who'd been in prison for over thirty years of his life now spend their lives serving others in our camp by doing all the laundry they can find for us, collecting the garbage, and by praying for others.

The majority of our residents, though, are in their thirties and had been on heroin an average of twelve years. They are on fire to reach others for Christ in practical and spiritual ways. All but a few have long prison records but there are no new entries on them now. They want to serve God in Hong Kong and China for the rest of their lives and are now running much of the ministry.

We pray regularly with street sleepers and beggars under the overpasses where they live. We take them rice, blankets, and clothes, and we expect to have words of knowledge to help in ministering to them. Every week complete strangers who have never before heard about Jesus are touched, healed, and believe in Christ. They are filled with the power of his Spirit at this time and begin to use spiritual gifts. Those who come to the Walled City inquiring about our drug withdrawal program are rarely in the room longer than five minutes before they pray to receive Christ and the Spirit comes on them. Our problem is that we cannot take them into our houses quickly enough, as there is a waiting list. However, as they decide to repent and while waiting to enter our houses even those still on heroin will be used to pray for others and prophesy.

Uncertain Future

The year 1986 was like a biblical Jubilee for us. We housed over 150 people and fed hundreds more weekly. Then the Hong Kong government offered us another house. It's a beautiful old colonial house in a scenic spot by the sea. There we can take in up to forty people coming off heroin. However, the queue of those waiting grows and grows. We could run ten more houses and still not keep up with all those who want to be changed by Jesus, because they've seen how Jesus changed their friends. We can't stop people coming to Christ; the word is out. He saves; he is good news.

Hong Kong's future is uncertain. It is officially returned to Chinese rule in 1997. In January 1987 it was announced that the Walled City itself will be pulled down in three years and the people resettled. We see that a squalid city that was known as "darkness" has now become famous for light, as all over Hong Kong people are drawn to it because that's where they find the Jesus who heals, feeds, houses, delivers, and forgives. And the people who carry the good news are the ones who've been healed, fed, housed, delivered, and forgiven. That's the gospel.

Afterword

In the introduction I traced the historical development of the Third Wave, pointing out the dramatic numerical growth of both modern Pentecostalism and the charismatic renewal. Depending on whose figures are quoted, there are between 178 and 277 million Pentecostals and charismatics worldwide.

The contributors to this book are a part of what C. Peter Wagner describes as the Third Wave of the Holy Spirit's work in this century. Now that you have read their stories I would like to reflect further on the meaning of the Third Wave and make a few observations on where it could be going.

In my book *Power Evangelism* I describe the Third Wave as "the next stage of development in the charismatic renewal. . . . [All three waves] are part of one great movement of the Holy Spirit in this century" (p. 122). And, while "the similarities between the movements outweigh their differences," there are real differences. What are those differences? To answer that question we must take a closer look at the first two waves. For each wave I will answer three questions:

- What is the doorway to a deeper experience of the life of the Holy Spirit?
- What theological explanation is offered for the experience?
- What are the expected results of the experience?

The First Wave

The First Wave, Pentecostalism, has a clearly defined experience, theology, and result. Classical Pentecostals believe that through experiencing "the baptism of the Holy Spirit" Christians receive the Third Person of the Trinity. Further, many believe the initial evidence of the baptism of the Holy Spirit is *always* speaking in tongues.

For many classical Pentecostals the baptism of the Holy Spirit means the Christian has been sanctified, or made holy, and thus will not sin any longer. This idea comes from Wesleyan-Arminian theology, which (among other things) says that Christians in this life are able to attain a state of such conformity to the divine will of God that they may be called perfect. Another group of Pentecostals—the Assemblies of God denomination being the most notable example—believe the baptism of the Holy Spirit is more for "empowering for service" than for sanctification. (I describe in detail the development of Pentecostalism in this century in chapter 9 of *Power Evangelism*.)

The result of this First Wave is that modern Pentecostalism is one of the most effective evangelistic and church growth forces in church history. C. Peter Wagner estimates that in 1985 there were 85 million members worldwide, and David B. Barrett's latest estimate is 147 million denominational Pentecostals worldwide. This is remarkable growth, and there are no signs of the growth letting up.

For example, Peter Wagner reports that in 1986 the Vision of the Future Church in Argentina, pastored by Omar Cabrera and his wife, Marfa, had 145,000 members, most of this growth coming in the last ten years. The church meets in 45 different locations, with Pastor Cabrera traveling over 7,000 miles a month to care for the flock. They are building a central meeting place in the city of Cordoba that will seat 17,000 people.

Another example of Pentecostal growth is found in Central America, an area that heretofore Protestants found difficult to have an impact on. With Pentecostals leading the way, Nicaragua (under the Marxist Sandinistas) has grown from 3 percent evangelicals in 1979 to 12 percent in 1983, and researcher Clifton Holland estimated the figure at 20 percent in 1986. In Guatemala evangelicals comprise over 25 percent of the population, again with Pentecostals in the majority. To these examples I could add many others; trends in Africa and Asia are just as impressive as in Latin America.

The Second Wave

The Second Wave, the charismatic renewal, is less clearly defined in the minds of the participants than is the First Wave. For example,

The Life in the Spirit Seminars, one of the most common teaching vehicles through which people have entered the charismatic renewal, speaks of *"being baptized* in the Holy Spirit" rather than *"the baptism* of the Holy Spirit." The former expression emphasizes the dynamic process of experiencing the Holy Spirit. The team manual for the Catholic edition of *The Life in the Spirit Seminars* says, "[Being baptized in the Holy Spirit] is not our first reception of the Holy Spirit, but a release of his power that is already within us through baptism and confirmation" (p. 114). Unlike classical Pentecostals, most charismatics do not insist on tongues as an evidence of being baptized in the Holy Spirit: ". . . we should make it clear that speaking in tongues is neither a necessary sign, nor by itself a certain sign, that a person has been baptized in the Spirit" (p. 143). Nevertheless, "everyone should want to have tongues" (p. 143).

Because the charismatic renewal is a movement of the Holy Spirit among a variety of denominations, there are a variety of theologies used to describe the experience of being baptized in the Holy Spirit. For example, the book *Welcome, Holy Spirit,* edited by Larry Christenson, offers answers to critical theological questions from a Lutheran perspective. Similar types of literature may be found in Catholic, Presbyterian, Episcopalian, and other mainline Protestant circles. Few of these explanations are rooted in Wesleyan-Arminian theology.

The charismatic renewal focuses on spiritual renewal of Christians within Catholic parishes and mainline churches. Church planting and evangelism outside of the churches is not a prominent feature of the Second Wave.

The Third Wave

The Third Wave, now twice removed from classical Pentecostalism, has a broad understanding of how Christians experience the power of the Holy Spirit. For example, the majority of Christians in the Third Wave do not use the terms "the baptism of the Holy Spirit" or "being baptized in the Holy Spirit." Instead, they speak of being "filled with the Holy Spirit" or, as I prefer to say, "empowered by the

Holy Spirit." Terminology is important, for it embodies the thinking that lies behind experience. In this case, members of the Third Wave define their encounters with the Holy Spirit as a step—to be sure an important one—in the process of spiritual growth. So, while most members of the Third Wave describe an initial, dramatic encounter with the Holy Spirit (what most call a "life-changing experience"), they also see the need for continual fillings.

Another distinguishing mark of the Third Wave is its inclusion of those who do not speak in tongues, but otherwise practice power ministry—divine healing, deliverance, prophecy, and so on. Jack Deere and Charles Kraft are riding the crest of the Third Wave, and neither has spoken in tongues. Not one of the persons in this book emphasizes tongues speaking as the most prominent feature of their testimony, though most do exercise the gift. The majority of those touched by the Third Wave are conservative evangelicals, which is why many of them believe their experience is compatible with re-formed theology.

In February of 1987 Kevin Springer conducted a poll of 2,041 people who attended a healing conference at the Anaheim Vineyard Christian Fellowship. (He conducted the poll during the first session of the conference.) His purpose was to draw a sociological and the-ological profile of members of the Third Wave. One of the questions Kevin asked concerned the participants' understanding of "the bap-tism of (or in) the Holy Spirit." Of those who identified themselves as evangelicals (excluding all members of Vineyard churches, this sam-ple included 267 people), only 2.24 percent (6 people) checked the classical Pentecostal definition. Forty-five percent (121 participants) thought it was "an experience distinct from and subsequent to the Holy Spirit's work of regeneration in which the Christian is empow-ered for service and witness; this experience may or may not be ac-companied by speaking in tongues." The largest response, 49.06 percent (131 people), thought it was "the initial action of the Holy Spirit, which happens at the time of conversion, that incorporates an individual into the body of Christ. Any later experiences with the Holy Spirit are better called 'fillings.' "

I believe that over the next few years books will be published that define more clearly the theological implications of the Third Wave, demonstrating that it falls in line with historic orthodoxy. In many instances the key to understanding the Third Wave will be discovered by studying the forgotten writings of some of the greatest evangelicals from the nineteenth century. For example, Dwight L. Moody's book *Secret Power,* originally published in 1881, was recently rereleased. In the book, which will surprise many readers, Moody argues for the necessity of seeking the Holy Spirit's power in our lives and the need for "a definite experience of which one may and ought to know whether he has received it [the baptism with the Holy Spirit] or not" (p. 137). Moody identified the source of his power and success as the Holy Spirit.

The Third Wave has many results similar to classical Pentecostalism and the charismatic renewal: evangelism, church planting, and the renewal of existing congregations are the most obvious. But I believe there is one result that may separate the Third Wave from the first two waves. If I am one of the leaders of the Third Wave, and if the ministry of the Vineyard is characteristic of where the Third Wave is going, then it is an equipping wave. By "equipping" I mean it is a wave in which *all* Christians are encouraged to pray for the sick and experience *all* the gifts. This is why I conduct training seminars, not healing campaigns; my goal is to release the healing ministry throughout the entire body, not keep it confined to only a few faith healers.

The emphasis on equipping the saints is in line with the teachings of reformers like Martin Luther and Philip Spener (the seventeenth-century founder of German Pietism). In volume 40 of his *Works,* Luther writes, "all Christians are priests, and all priests are Christians" (p. 19). The universal priesthood of all believers received even more attention from Spener, as he writes in his book, *Pia Desideria:* "not only ministers but all Christians are made priests by their Savior, are anointed by the Holy Spirit, and are dedicated to perform spiritual-priestly acts" (p. 92).

The emphasis on equipping the saints is not as far removed from the first two waves as it may appear. In the First Wave, Pentecostals were excluded from most conservative evangelical seminaries and Bible schools. Because a majority of Pentecostals came from economically and educationally disadvantaged classes of people, most of their leadership training was done outside a classroom setting and in the field. This system of leadership training may not have produced the best Bible scholars and theologians, but their "home grown" pastors have been the most successful at evangelism and church growth in this century. Still, in the First Wave the focus on ministry and equipping was largely limited to professional pastors; other Christians only incidentally received this type of training.

The Second Wave, the charismatic renewal, is built on a system of lay leaders: prayer group leaders, Bible study leaders, cell group leaders, small group leaders, and so on. The training focus for lay leaders is how to pastor people and help them grow in Christian character. In a few instances this emphasis created introverted, authoritarian groups. This is perhaps a contributing factor to the recent slowdown in growth in some parts of the charismatic renewal.

The Third Wave is a reforming movement of the training system found in most churches in Western culture. It is moving the ministry from the pulpit to the pews, from clergy to laity, from the few to the many. Instead of training only pastor-evangelists, healer-evangelists, or small group pastors, the Third Wave is training all Christians for power ministry, especially personal evangelism and divine healing. Of course, the harvest that this produces creates the need for more pastors and lay leaders, and that type of training continues in the Third Wave.

The Third Wave emphasizes the universal priesthood of all Christians, not just those whose stories appear in this book. The only requirements for riding that wave are a hunger for God and a humility to receive him on his terms. Your power encounter is only as far away as this prayer: "Holy Spirit, I open my heart, my innermost being to you. I turn from my sin and self-sufficiency and ask that you fill me with your love, power, and gifts. Come, Holy Spirit."

JOHN WIMBER

Bibliography

Becker, Carl. *The Heavenly City of the Eighteenth-Century Philosophers*. New Haven, CN: Yale University, 1932.

Bennett, Dennis. *Nine O'Clock in the Morning*. Plainfield, NJ: Logos, 1970.

Bennett, Dennis and Rita. *The Holy Spirit and You*. Plainfield, NJ: Logos, 1971.

Bloesch, Donald G. *Essentials of Evangelical Theology*. Vol. 2. San Francisco: Harper & Row, 1978.

Bloom, Allan. *The Closing of the American Mind*. New York: Simon & Schuster, 1987.

Bruner, Frederick Dale. *A Theology of the Holy Spirit: The Pentecostal Experience and the New Testament*. Grand Rapids, MI: Eerdmans, 1970.

Christenson, Larry. *Welcome Holy Spirit*. Minneapolis, MN: Bethany, 1987.

Johnston, Robert K., ed. *The Use of the Bible in Theology—Evangelical Options*. Atlanta, GA: John Knox, 1985.

Kraft, Charles. *Christianity in Culture*. Maryknoll, NY: Orbis, 1979.

The Life in the Spirit Seminars. Team Manual, Catholic Edition. Ann Arbor, MI: Servant, 1973.

Lindsell, Harold. *The New Paganism*. San Francisco: Harper & Row, 1987.

Luther, Martin. *Luther's Works*. St. Louis, MO: Concordia, 1958.

Mallone, George. *Those Controversial Gifts*. Downers Grove, IL: Inter-Varsity Press, 1983.

Moody, Dwight L. *Secret Power*. Ventura, CA: Gospel Light, 1987.

Newbigin, Lesslie. *Foolishness to the Greeks*. Grand Rapids, MI: Eerdmans, 1986.

Pullinger, Jackie. *Chasing the Dragon*. Ann Arbor, MI: Servant, 1980.

Pytches, David. *Come, Holy Spirit.* London: Hodder & Stoughton, 1985.

Pytches, Mary. *Set My People Free.* London: Hodder & Stoughton, 1986.

Spener, Philip Jacob. *Pia Desideria.* Ed. and trans. Theodore G. Tappert. Philadelphia, PA: Fortress, 1964.

Tippett, Alan R. *People Movements in Southern Polynesia.* Chicago: Moody, 1971.

———. *Solomon Islands Christianity.* Pasadena, CA: Wm. Carey Library, 1967.

Virgo, Terry. *Restoration in the Church.* Eastbourne: Kingsway Publications, 1985.

Wagner, C. Peter. *Spiritual Power and Church Growth.* Altamonte Springs, FL: Creation House, 1987.

Watson, David. *Fear No Evil.* London: Hodder & Stoughton, 1984.

Wimber, John, with Kevin Springer. *Power Evangelism.* San Francisco: Harper & Row, 1986.

———. *Power Healing.* San Francisco: Harper & Row, 1987.